BERKLEE PRESS

PIANO ESSENTIALS

Scales, Chords, Arpeggios, and Cadences for the Contemporary Pianist

To access audio visit:
www.halleonard.com/mylibrary

Enter Code
3795-5494-9666-7744

ROSS RAMSAY

Edited by Susan Gedutis Lindsay

Berklee Media

Vice President: Dave Kusek
Dean of Continuing Education: Debbie Cavalier
Director of Business Affairs: Robert Green
Associate Director of Technology: Mike Serio
Marketing Manager, Berkleemusic: Barry Kelly
Senior Graphic Designer: Robert Heath

Berklee Press

Senior Writer/Editor: Jonathan Feist
Production Manager: Shawn Girsberger
Marketing Manager, Berklee Press: Jennifer D'Angora

Special thanks to Meghan C. Joyce and Louis Ochoa for editorial and production support.

ISBN: 978-0-87639-049-8

Printed in the United States of America
13 12 11 10 09 08 07 06   6 5 4 3 2 1

 Berklee Press

1140 Boylston Street
Boston, MA 02215-3693 USA
(617) 747-2146
Visit Berklee Press Online at
www.berkleepress.com

DISTRIBUTED BY
 HAL•LEONARD®
7777 W. BLUEMOUND RD. P.O. BOX 13819
MILWAUKEE, WISCONSIN 53213
Visit Hal Leonard Online at
www.halleonard.com

Contents

Audio Track List

The accompanying audio includes examples of many of the exercises in this book. As you read through the book, you'll see track numbers and an audio icon in the outside margin of the page. Listen to those tracks to hear examples of the materials being presented.

The audio includes demonstrations of how to work on various exercises in the book. Listen or play along with tracks 1–24 as I play all major scales at 60 and 100 beats per minute (BPM). You can also practice any of the exercises in this book with the rhythm tracks provided on tracks 30–33; an example of this is provided on track 29.

Track

1 C major (60 BPM)

2 G major (60 BPM)

3 D major (60 BPM)

4 A major (60 BPM)

5 E major (60 BPM)

6 B major (60 BPM)

7 F♯ major (60 BPM)

8 D♭ major (60 BPM)

9 A♭ major (60 BPM)

10 E♭ major (60 BPM)

11 B♭ major (60 BPM)

12 F major (60 BPM)

13 C major (100 BPM)

14 G major (100 BPM)

15 D major (100 BPM)

16 A major (100 BPM)

17 E major (100 BPM)

18 B major (100 BPM)

19 F♯ major (100 BPM)

Track

20 D♭ major (100 BPM)

21 A♭ major (100 BPM)

22 E♭ major (100 BPM)

23 B♭ major (100 BPM)

24 F major (100 BPM)

25 Dynamic gradations, exercises A, B, C, D in key of C

26 Articulation and phrasing exercise 1A; staccato, C major scale, and arpeggio in one, two, three, and four octaves, with rhythmic groupings of quarter, eighth, eighth-note triplet, and sixteenth notes (pg. 48)

27 Articulation and phrasing exercises 2A, 2B, 2C: staccato and legato (pg. 49)

28 Four-octave C major scale with rhythmic contrast exercises 1, 2, 3, 4 (pg. 55)

29 Listening example: Major scales and arpeggios played with rhythm track from track 32

30 Latin drum rhythms (70 BPM)

31 Funk drum rhythms (80 BPM)

32 Funk drum rhythms (96 BPM)

33 Swing drum rhythms (130 BPM)

Introduction

Music is the combination of melody, harmony, and rhythm. This book will help you improve your keyboard skills in all three of these areas by focusing on the study of scales, chords, arpeggios, and cadences. The scales and arpeggios presented in this book are part of the minimum requirements of every Level 1 and Level 2 Berklee College of Music piano student, and students wishing to advance their performance skills will be well served by these studies.

Music is an expressive language, and by practicing structures that are common to all tonal forms of song, your ability to communicate in that language is greatly enhanced. If you master the exercises in this book, you will find that your sight-reading skills improve because you have learned many of the most common melodic and harmonic patterns upon which music is built. Familiarity with these basic patterns will also help you memorize new material in less time and with more confidence. Mastering each of these exercises in all keys provides an important grounding upon which to build advanced study of the keyboard.

How to Use This Book

To get the most from this book, you should know how to read music and should have some knowledge of the keyboard.

I have organized the material to follow a natural progression of scale and arpeggio study, and related theory. We begin with some basic concepts that are critical to fully understanding more advanced theory. For many students, these basics will serve as a helpful review.

This book is divided into four parts. Part I includes Berklee College of Music Level 1 Piano Department technique requirements, and part II covers rhythm and expression. Part III provides reference information on minor scales so that you can use the exercises in parts I and II to explore minor, fulfilling Berklee Level 2 Piano Department technique requirements. Part IV provides key-area studies, more advanced concepts, and additional technique exercises.

The art of piano playing is a lifelong journey; let this book serve as a reference to challenge you for years to come.

Berklee College of Music Piano Technique Requirements

LEVEL 1

- All major scales and arpeggios in four rhythmic groupings of quarter, eighth, eighth triplet, and sixteenth notes, for 1, 2, 3, and 4 octaves each.

- All major I IV V I and I VI II V I cadences with all inversions.

LEVEL 2

- Harmonic, traditional melodic, and jazz melodic minor scales and arpeggios in four rhythmic groupings of quarter, eighth, eighth triplet, and sixteenth notes, for 1, 2, 3, and 4 octaves each.

- All minor I IV V I and I VI II V I cadences with all inversions.

Technique Overview

Technical facility comes from improving the balance of mechanical activities used in piano playing—not by overemphasizing and, subsequently, overstressing a single muscle group. You must learn to balance all parts of the body used in piano playing, including fingers, wrists, forearms, upper arms, shoulders, neck, torso, legs, and feet, all working together to enable the most efficient use of energy.

The scales, arpeggios, and musical exercises in this book are much more than just "finger exercises." As you practice, always remember that while the fingers are the structure that makes physical contact with the keys, the rest of the body also brings them into play so that they are not forced to work or stretch unnecessarily. This will be most apparent when you attempt multiple-octave arpeggios, and as you increase the tempos in all examples.

I highly encourage further study of piano technique, and working with a good teacher is very important. In addition, here are two books that I have found thought-provoking: *On Piano Playing* by Abby Whiteside (Amadeus Press) and *On Piano Playing* by Gyorgy Sandor (Schirmer Books). Also check out other Berklee Press titles written by Berklee piano faculty.

Proper Playing Posture

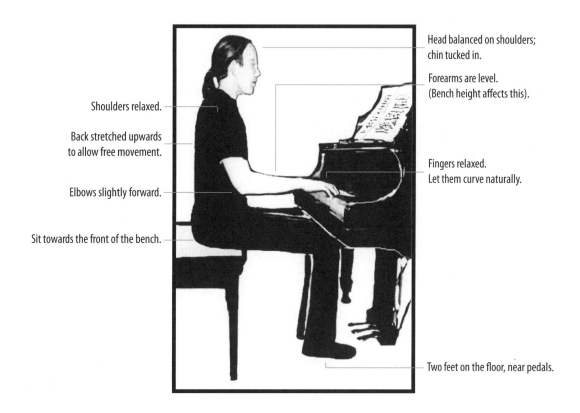

Shoulders relaxed.

Back stretched upwards to allow free movement.

Elbows slightly forward.

Sit towards the front of the bench.

Head balanced on shoulders; chin tucked in.

Forearms are level. (Bench height affects this).

Fingers relaxed. Let them curve naturally.

Two feet on the floor, near pedals.

Practice Routines

Here are some tips on planning your practice sessions:

■ Schedule practice times into your routine; don't expect to "eventually get to it."

■ Be consistent. Forty-five minutes every day is more productive than trying to practice five hours on Sunday.

■ Plan your practice session. Having goals for each week allows a clear focus during practice time.

Here are two examples of possible practice routines.

If you have forty-five minutes per day:

15 min.	Begin learning first page of a new song
10 min.	Scales, arpeggios, and exercises in two keys
20 min.	Finish last week's song, adding more dynamics, and memorize first page

If you have two hours a day:

15 min.	Sight reading
15 min.	Harmonic minor scales and arpeggios in three keys
25 min.	Finish notated music piece, focus on phrasing, dynamics, and fingerings
5 min.	Stretch break
15 min.	Cadences (I IV V I and I VI II V I)
15 min.	Jazz lead sheet practice, focusing on voice leading chords in steady rhythm
15 min.	Improvisation on a common progression
15 min.	Transcription of recorded piano solo or jazz lead sheet

Of course, this schedule will vary, depending on upcoming performances or recitals, but it gives you a general approach to structuring a practice session.

PART I

Scale Studies in Major Keys

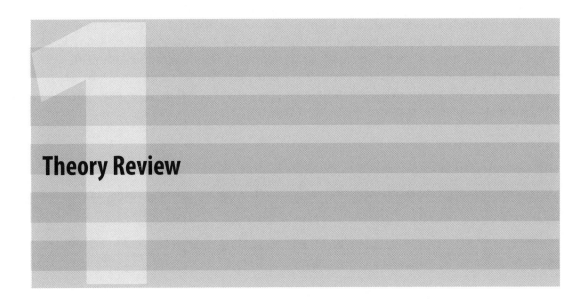

Theory Review

Let's begin with a review of music theory. Whether you are new to music theory or are well versed, I encourage you to read this section so that you can familiarize yourself with important terms and concepts used in this book.

Scales

A scale is a series of pitches arranged in either ascending or descending order. There are many possible scales. The major scale is one of the most common. The major scale can be formulated by measuring the distances between the notes in half steps or whole steps. One half step is the distance between any two immediately adjacent keys on the keyboard, whether white or black. One whole step is movement by two half steps.

Here is the formula of whole steps and half steps for a major scale:

Whole – Whole – Half – Whole – Whole – Whole – Half

Applying the above whole-step/half-step formula to any starting note creates a major scale and a key unique to it. The key is identified by a key signature, which appears on the staff between the clef sign and the time signature. The key signature identifies the sharps or flats that appear in the scale. For example, with a starting note of E♭, the whole-step/half-step formula yields a major scale with three flats. The key signature of E♭ indicates that the flats are B♭, E♭, and A♭.

Here are all twelve major key signatures. The keys are arranged moving clockwise by five scale steps; this is called the circle of fifths, or Cycle 5:

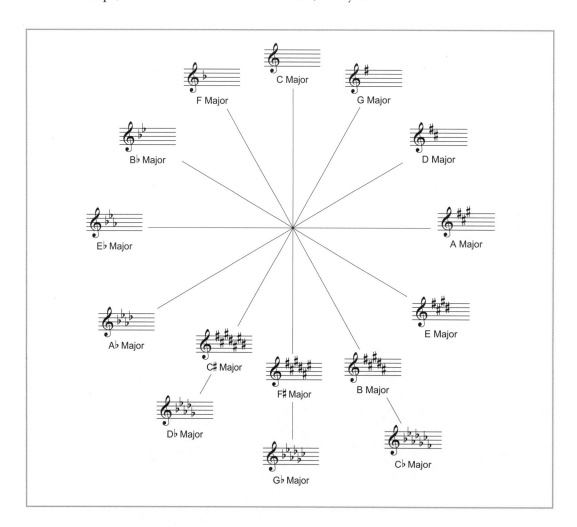

Songs written in a particular key signature are built primarily of notes found in that scale.

Notice that all major scales always have one and only one of each note from the musical alphabet (A, B, C, D, E, F, G). These notes may be either sharped or flatted—but never both!

Intervals and Chords

An interval is the distance between two notes. The example below shows all the possible intervals contained within one octave. Each interval is one half step greater than the prior interval. (Remember, two half steps equal one whole step.)

In the diagram below, each interval is built from the starting note (tonic) of middle C. Play each interval one note at a time, and then together, listening to how it sounds. Try playing these same intervals starting at various notes on the keyboard.

There are five kinds of intervals: perfect, major, minor, diminished, and augmented.

- Intervals of a fourth and fifth above the tonic in a major scale are called "perfect."

- A perfect interval lowered by a half step becomes "diminished."

- A major interval lowered by one half step becomes minor.

- A minor interval lowered by one half step becomes diminished.

- Both perfect and major intervals become "augmented" when raised by one half step.

Playing three or more notes simultaneously forms a chord. Triads are three-note chords whose adjacent intervals are either major or minor thirds. The starting pitch is referred to as the root of the chord. Here is a C major triad. It is formed by adjacent intervals of a major third and minor third.

Another way to create a major triad is by combining the first, third, and fifth note of a major scale.

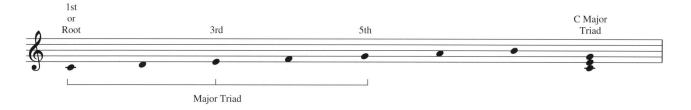

Once you have formed a major triad, you can make it minor by lowering the third one half step. To make a major triad into a diminished one, lower the third and the fifth by a half step. To make it augmented, raise the fifth by a half step. Four triad possibilities are shown below, built around the starting pitch of middle C.

Scale degrees: Each note in the scale is given a number, called a scale degree, that represents its order (ascending) from the starting note. The starting note, also known as the "tonic" or "root," is always scale degree 1. Scale degrees are normally labeled with Arabic numerals, and the chords that are built on these scale degrees are labeled with corresponding Roman numerals. (You will learn more about building chords on each of these scale degrees in chapter 2.)

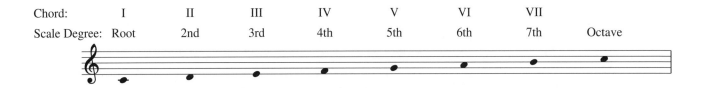

Be careful not to confuse intervals with scale degrees when analyzing music. As an example, the fourth and sixth scale degrees of C major are F and A, but the interval between them is a major third.

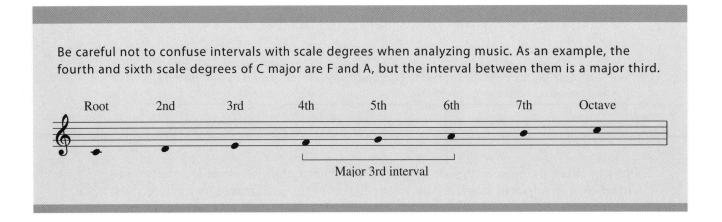

Triads can be played in three positions: root position, first inversion, and second inversion. When the starting note, or root, of the triad is at the bottom of the chord, the triad is in root position. Raising the root to the top of the voicing, leaving the third as the bottom note, creates first inversion. Raising the third to the top of the voicing, leaving the fifth as the bottom note, creates second inversion. These inversions are shown here in the key of C:

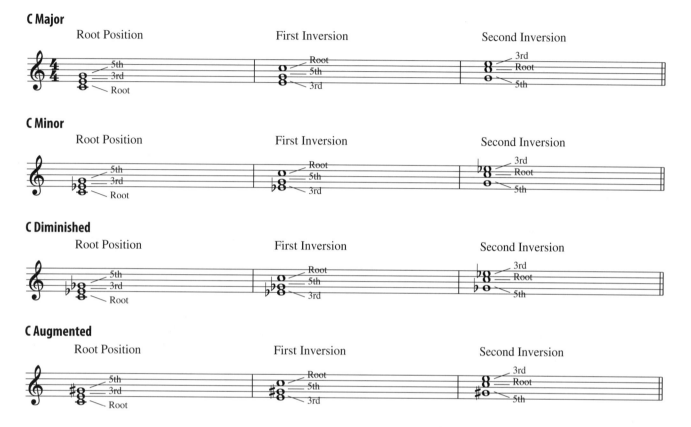

C Major

C Minor

C Diminished

C Augmented

Arpeggios

Playing the notes of a chord in succession rather than all at once forms an arpeggio. Here are arpeggios for four chords:

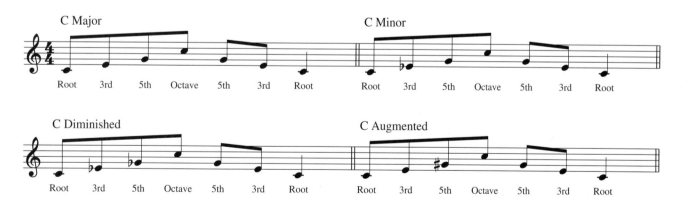

About Chord Symbols

Chord symbols may be written several ways. Here are different chord symbols for major, minor, augmented, and diminished. All of these are correct. This book generally uses the one listed in bold.

C major	**C**	C♯Maj	CM	CΔ
C minor	**C–**	C♯min	Cm	
C augmented	**C+**	C Aug		
C diminished	**C°**	C Dim		

EXERCISES Major Scales, Arpeggios, and Triad Inversions of I Major

In the exercises on the following pages, you'll work on major scales and chords. Practice each exercise slowly at first, and always use the correct fingering. Being inconsistent with notes and fingerings leads to inconsistent and mistake-filled performances. You are teaching your body new movements that may seem foreign and awkward at first, but at some point, these movements will become natural and will happen effortlessly.

Memorizing the scales and arpeggios will allow you to easily recall what you have learned and apply it to the music you are working on. Also, make sure to memorize the key signature associated with each scale. Recognizing the key will make sight-reading much easier.

NOTE: As a point of reference, both F♯ and G♭ scales are included here, even though both scales have identical fingerings and pitches (though named differently). The two scales are called enharmonic equivalents. Likewise, C♯ is identical in fingering to D♭, and C♭ is identical in fingering to B. These enharmonic equivalents are not repeated in future exercises.

Also, note the arpeggio fingerings in the keys of A♭, B♭, E♭, D♭, and C♯. In these keys, the fingering for one-octave arpeggios can be accomplished more easily with 1, 2, 3, 5 (right hand) and 5, 3, 2, 1 (left hand), but *the arpeggio fingerings given here for those particular keys are different*, in order to prepare you for working with multiple-octave arpeggios.

As you practice songs, look for scales and arpeggios as they appear in the music. It is much easier to think of a group of notes as a whole than as individual pitches. For example, it is easier to recognize a passage as an octave and a half of a G major scale, rather than as the individual pitches G, A, B, C, D, E, F♯, G, A, B, C, D.

C Major

G Major

D Major

A Major

E Major

B Major

F♯ Major

C♯ Major

C♭ Major

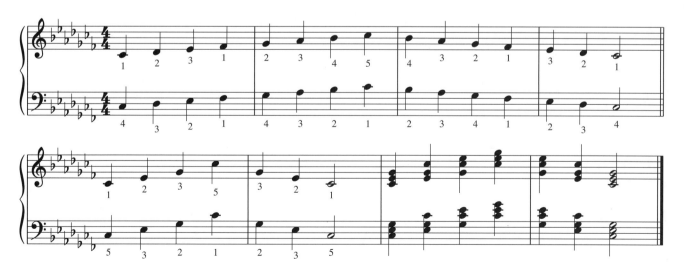

G♭ Major

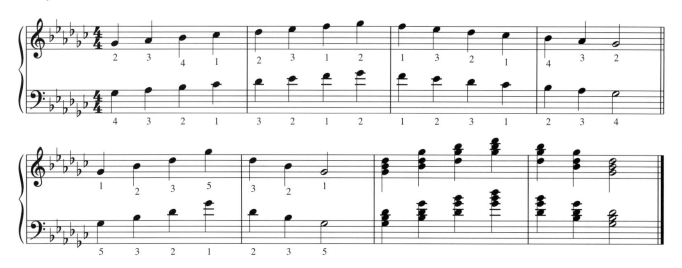

D♭ Major

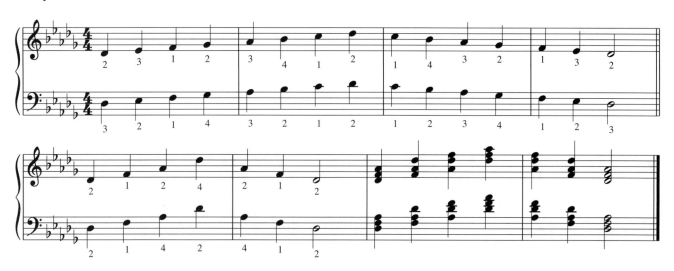

A♭ Major

E♭ Major

B♭ Major

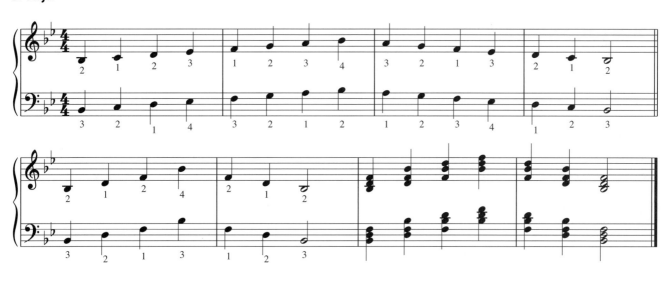

F Major

About Listening...

Music is an art for the ears. Training your ears to listen carefully is an important part of being a musician. Listen to the pitch of each note in the scale as you play it. Try hitting the first note and singing (or humming) the remaining notes. If you are having difficulty singing the whole scale, try singing just the note that follows the last one you played. Training your ears to hear what you are about to play will greatly increase your confidence at the instrument and will open the door to improvisation.

Diatonic Triads

Notes that occur within a given key are said to be diatonic to that key.

For example, C, D, E, F, G, A, and B are the diatonic notes to the key of C major. These are the *only* notes that are diatonic to the key of C major. Any chord that is formed from these notes is diatonic to the key of C major.

We can start from any note of the major scale and, using only notes of that major scale, build upwards in intervals of thirds to form triads. These chords are called diatonic triads. Diatonic triads are chords build entirely of notes from a single key.

The chord qualities of each diatonic triad (major, minor, or diminished) are consistent from key to key:

Scale Degree of Root	Roman Numeral	Chord Quality
1	I	major
2	II	minor
3	III	minor
4	IV	major
5	V	major
6	VI	minor
7	VII	diminished

Diatonic Chord Construction Based on the C Major Scale:

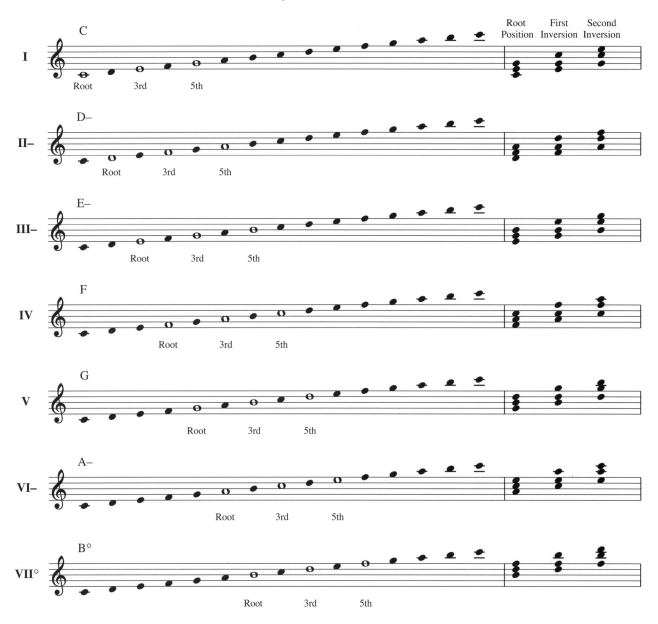

EXERCISES Diatonic Triads

Play through the diatonic triads for each key as notated. Remember, the chord qualities (major, minor, diminished) of each scale degree are the same from key to key. Keeping the key signature in mind as you play will help. Practice it with both hands together (one triad per hand, one octave apart), and with each hand separately.

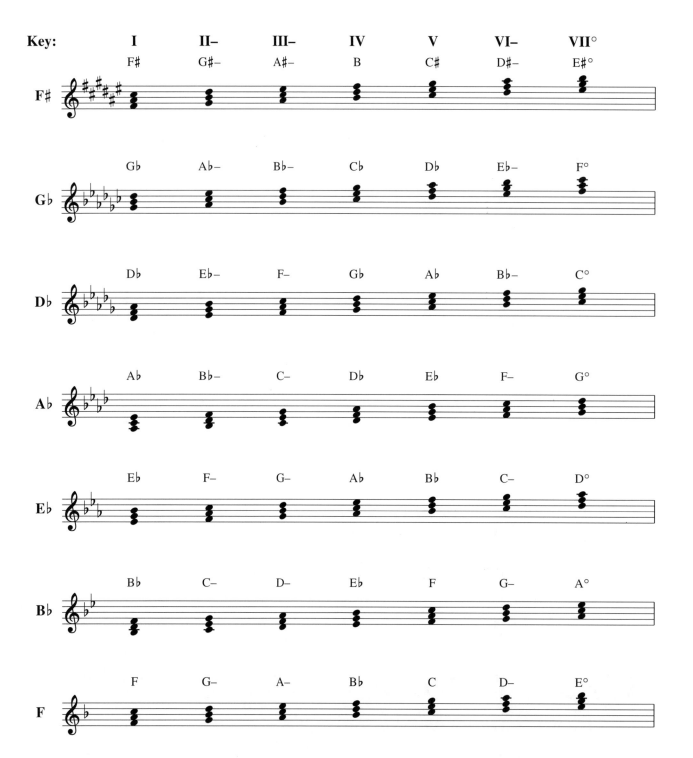

EXERCISES Diatonic Triads

These exercises outline diatonic triads, ascending and descending through each chord, and serve as good warm-up exercises. The fingerings provided work for all keys. Try coming up with pattern variations of your own. Keep a list of what keys and what exercises you have done, working towards feeling comfortable in all keys. Beginners may want to focus on one or two keys per week. Remember to play each note clearly and maintain a consistent volume throughout the exercise. Practice these exercises in a range of tempos, but do not play any faster than you are capable of: **speed and accuracy are only developed by mistake-free practicing**.

Use the fingering in each first measure for the entire exercise.

1.

Challenge

Practice all the chords in each key using all first-inversion chords, and then all second-inversion chords. It may be helpful at first to play the root of the chord in the left hand while playing the inversion of the chord in the right. Here are examples in the key of C. Work towards mastering all inversions in all keys. Use the appropriate major scale fingering for the left hand.

1. C Major first inversion diatonic triads

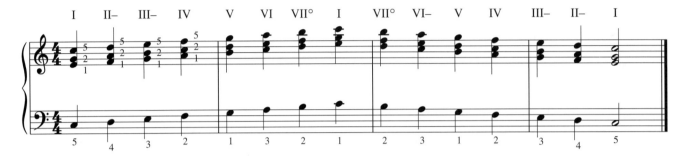

2. C major second inversion diatonic triads

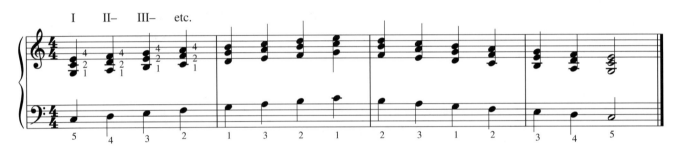

Chord Progressions:
Two-Octave Major Scales and Arpeggios

After playing the chords consecutively in any given key, try moving randomly from one chord to another, staying within a single key. You will probably find that many of the combinations sound familiar. A pattern of movement from chord to chord is known as a chord progression. Play the chord progressions below in the key of C and try naming a few of the thousands of songs written with them!

Progression 1

Progression 2

It is important to learn chord progressions in all keys. Professional musicians can play songs in any key because they understand what scales and chords the song is built from, and can translate this information freely from key to key. Try playing the above progressions, or some of your own, in different keys.

Here is the I IV V IV I progression in the key of E.

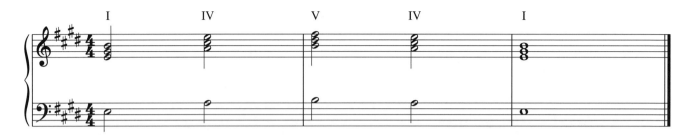

Here is a I VI– IV V I in the key of F.

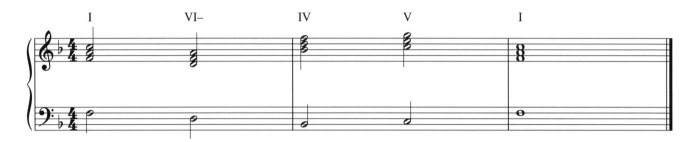

Cadences and Voice Leading

Cadences are chord progressions that typically create a sense of resolution. Play the following examples of common cadences, and experiment with various rhythms.

I IV V I Cadence

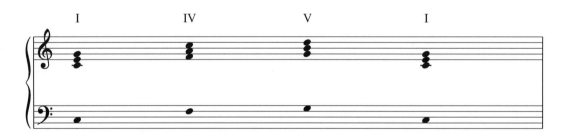

II V I Cadence

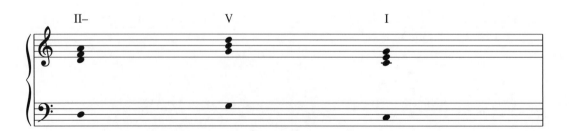

I VI II V I Cadence

As shown below, this chord progression jumps around the keyboard. You can mini-mize the amount of hand movement required between chords by inverting some of the chords, so that each voice moves to the closest possible note in the next chord. This creates a much smoother transition from chord to chord. This process is known as voice leading. Mastering all chord inversions will make voice leading effortless.

With No Voice Leading, All in Root Position

Root
Position

With Voice Leading Using Inversions, Starting from Root Position

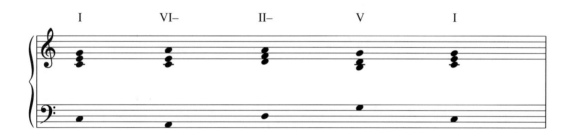

EXERCISES Cadences

Here are two cadences that are required of all Berklee Level 1 piano students. These cadences form the harmonic basis for many popular and jazz tunes. They are so common that having them under your fingertips will simplify learning and memorizing new material.

These cadences are notated with inversions for smooth voice leading. Memorize them in all keys, and always think of the key signature as you play. Look for these and other common cadences as you learn new songs.

> These cadences, shown below in the key of C, are to be played in all keys, starting from each position: root, first inversion, and second inversion of the I chord, as noted below.

I IV V I Cadence

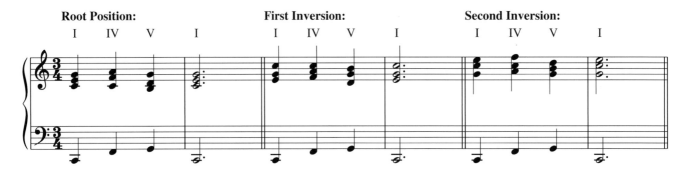

I VI– II– V I Cadence

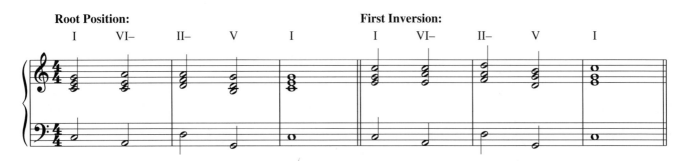

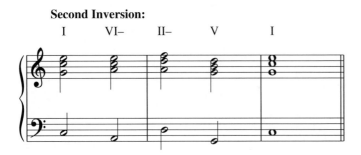

EXERCISES Major Scales and Arpeggios, Two Octaves

Once you can confidently play the major scales and arpeggios in one octave, start stretching your boundaries, aiming towards playing across the entire keyboard in a range of tempos. Playing them in two octaves is the next step. The only change in fingering from one-octave scales will be at the start of each new octave. As you practice, focus on rhythmic evenness and consistent articulation—not just on speed.

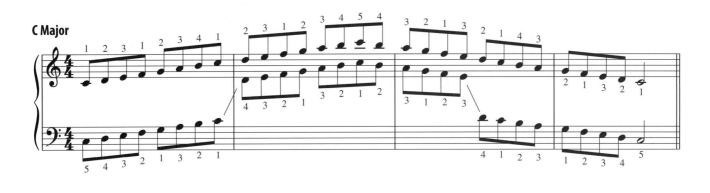

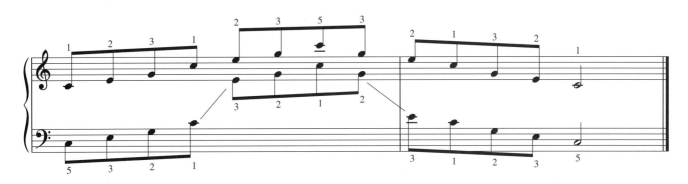

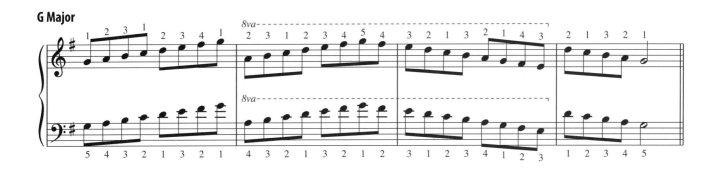

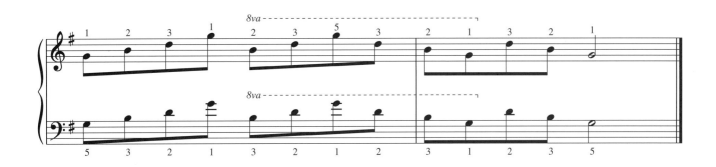

D Major

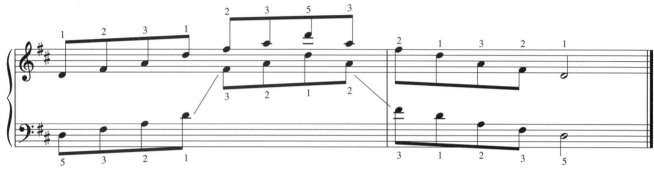

A Major

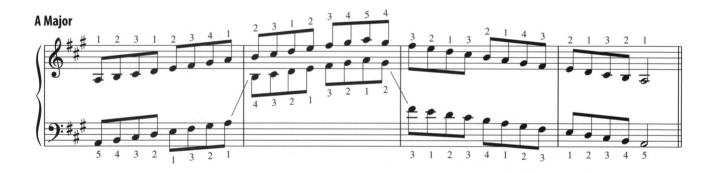

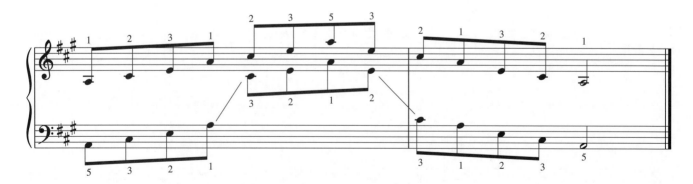

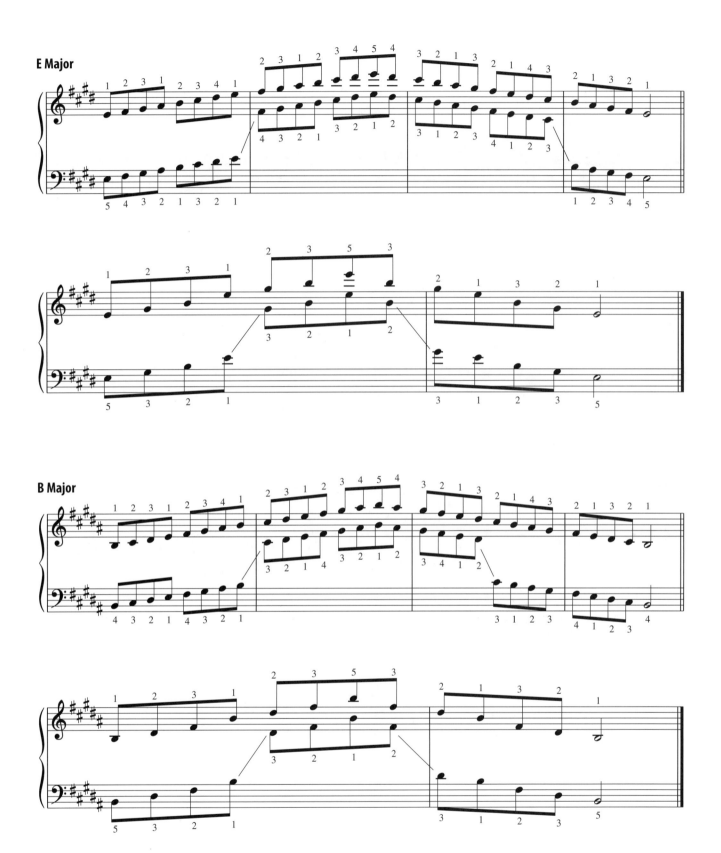

G♭ Major

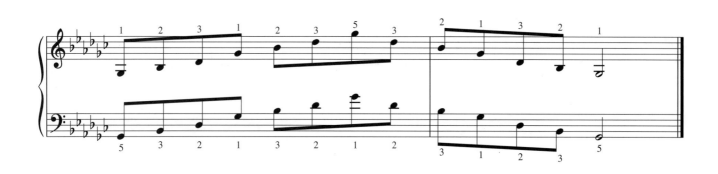

D♭ Major

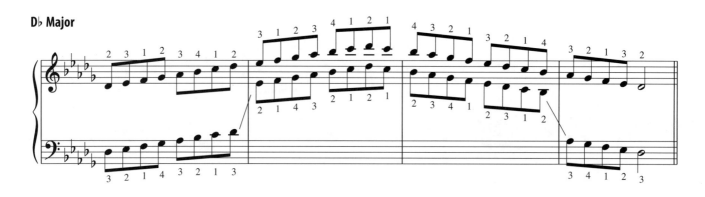

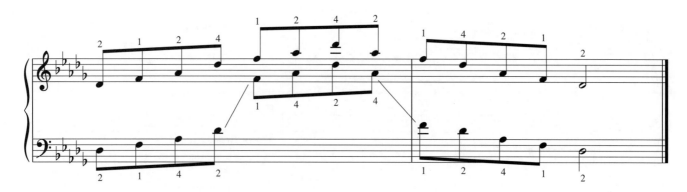

A♭ Major

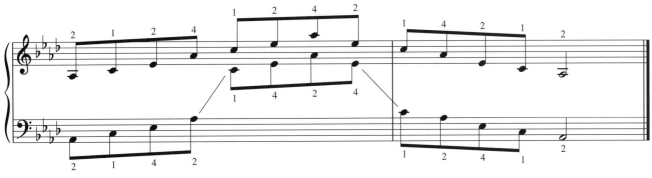

E♭ Major

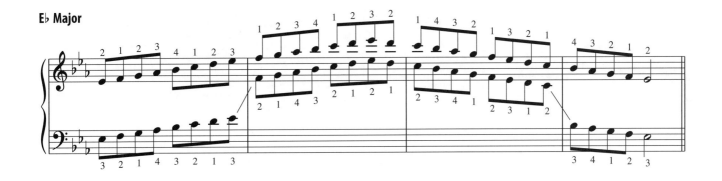

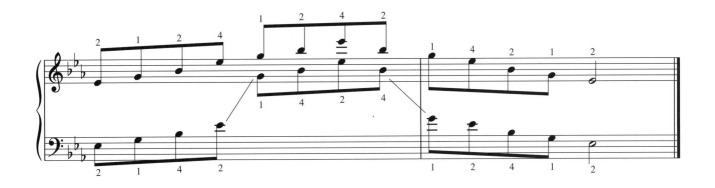

B♭ Major

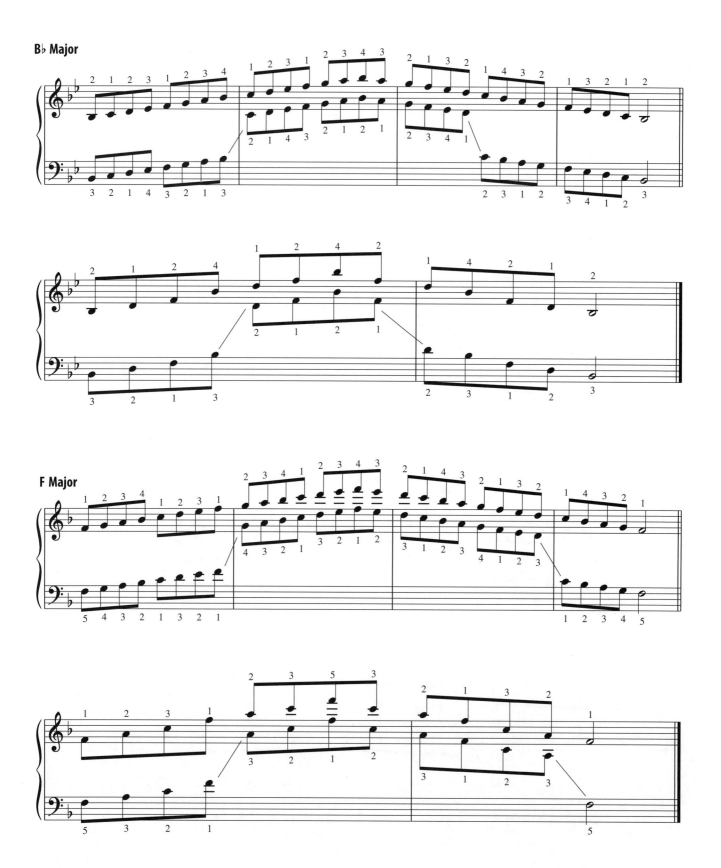

F Major

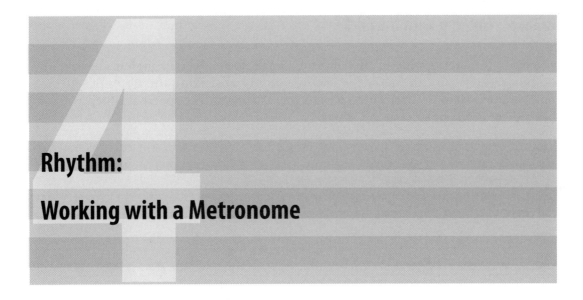

Rhythm:

Working with a Metronome

Rhythm is one of the most important elements of music; it brings music to life. To develop a sense of rhythm, work on scale and chord exercises with a metronome. The metronome offers an exact reference point to the tempo of the music, and helps develop an internal sense of pulse. In solo piano performance, there is greater flexibility with tempos, but there should always be an obvious sense of where the pulse is. As a studio musician, it is essential to be able to play precisely with a metronome or click track, because often the instrumentation is put together piece by piece, one player at a time, and the producer needs the musicians to sound as if they all recorded together.

Developing the ability to follow a metronome (and in doing so, developing your own internal sense of pulse) puts you in control of your performance. It's not that all music should be played without some freedom in pulse. Great performers use the ebb and flow of tempo as a very expressive tool—but they are always in control of it. Working with the metronome as you practice scales, arpeggios, and exercises will help develop your internal sense of pulse so you can play as accurately or freely as the musical situation requires.

EXERCISES Working with the Click

Begin by using the metronome to click on the quarter note. Play through each scale and see how closely you can follow the timing, aiming at striking the notes exactly as the metronome sounds. Start with a tempo that is close to the speed at which you have been successfully practicing the scale.

1. Major scale with metronome clicks on each beat

2. Two-octave major scale with eighth notes; metronome set to click on beat

Experiment with different tempos. Slower tempos are harder to follow because there is more time between clicks, leaving more chance for losing the pulse. Faster tempos are easier to follow, but more technically difficult to play. Identify what your limits are, and expand them: Can you play at 40 beats per minute (BPM) without losing the pulse? Can you smoothly play your scales and arpeggios two octaves in eighth notes at 120 BPM? Keep a record of the settings and track your progress.

EXERCISES Scales/Arpeggios with Rhythmic Groupings

After mastering the scales and arpeggios for one and two octaves, you can refine the physical technique as well as strengthen your mental perception of the varying rhythms by playing the scales and arpeggios for one, two, three, and four octaves, with rhythmic groupings of quarter, eighth, eighth triplet, and sixteenth notes. These groupings are the most common rhythmic subdivisions in all styles of music, so it is extremely important to be able to move accurately between them.

The example on the following pages is provided in the key of C. Play it in all keys and use the metronome to keep your tempo consistent between rhythmic subdivisions. As you get comfortable, challenge yourself by finding your tempo limits, both slow and fast, and gradually expand them as far as you can. No matter what speed you play, always maintain the accuracy of the notes and fingering. Master one key at a time, and keep track of your progress.

Listen to tracks 1–24 to hear examples of major scales and arpeggios played at 60 and 100 BPM. (See page v for a complete audio track list.)

1–24

1. Scales and arpeggios, four-octave rhythmic subdivisions

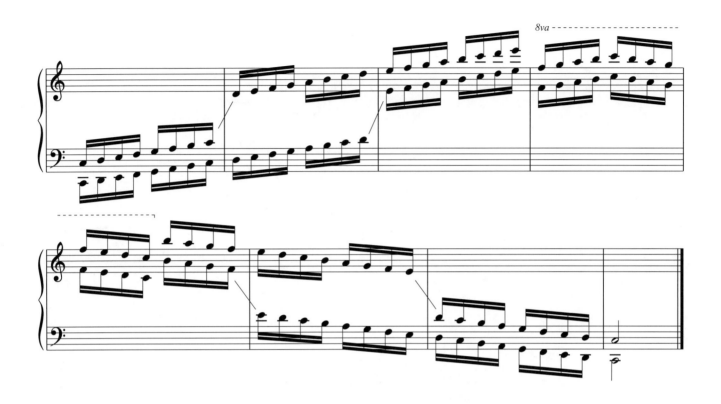

2.

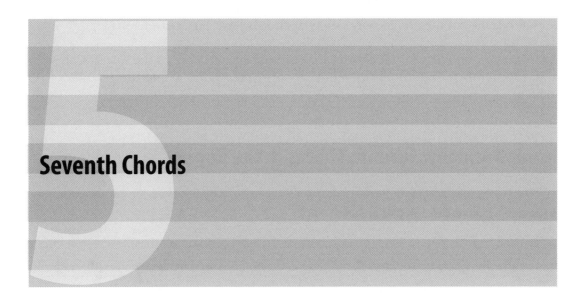

Seventh Chords

Adding the seventh scale degree to a triad results in a seventh chord. This creates richer-sounding harmonic textures, and opens up a number of chord possibilities. Play each of these seventh chords and listen to the sounds carefully.

Adding the seventh scale degree to the major triad forms a Major7 chord.

Adding the flatted seventh scale degree to a major triad forms a Dominant7 chord.

Adding the seventh scale degree to a minor triad forms a Minor/Major7 chord.

Adding the flatted seventh scale degree to a minor triad forms a Minor7 chord.

Adding the flatted seventh scale degree to a diminished triad forms a Minor7b5 chord.

Adding a double flatted seventh scale degree (lowered two half steps) to a diminished triad forms a Diminished7 chord.

Notice that because of the added note, seventh chords have three inversions.

Similar to triads, diatonic seventh chords are built using each note of the major scale as a root. (Remember: Diatonic chords contain only notes found within the given key signature.)

Diatonic Harmony: Seventh Chords in the Key of C

Diatonic Seventh Chord Construction Based on C Major Scale:

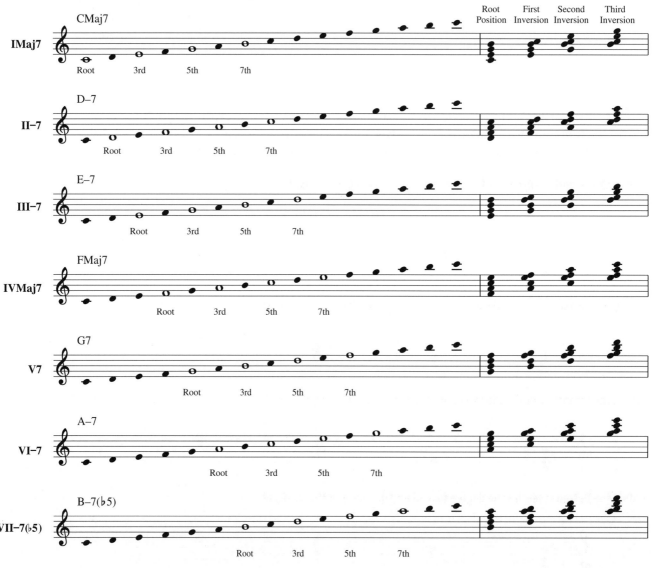

The chord **qualities** (major, minor, diminished, etc.) of the seventh chords built on each scale degree are identical, regardless of the key signature. For example, the chord built on the second scale degree of any major scale will always be a minor 7 chord, no matter what key it is in.

EXERCISES Root-Position Diatonic Seventh Chords in All Major Keys

Play through all the root-position diatonic seventh chords on this page and the next in each major key with the right hand, while playing only the root of the chord in the left. Once you can play through them in root position, play the exercise again with all first inversion chords, then second inversion, then third inversion chords, as in the "Challenge" exercises on page 20.

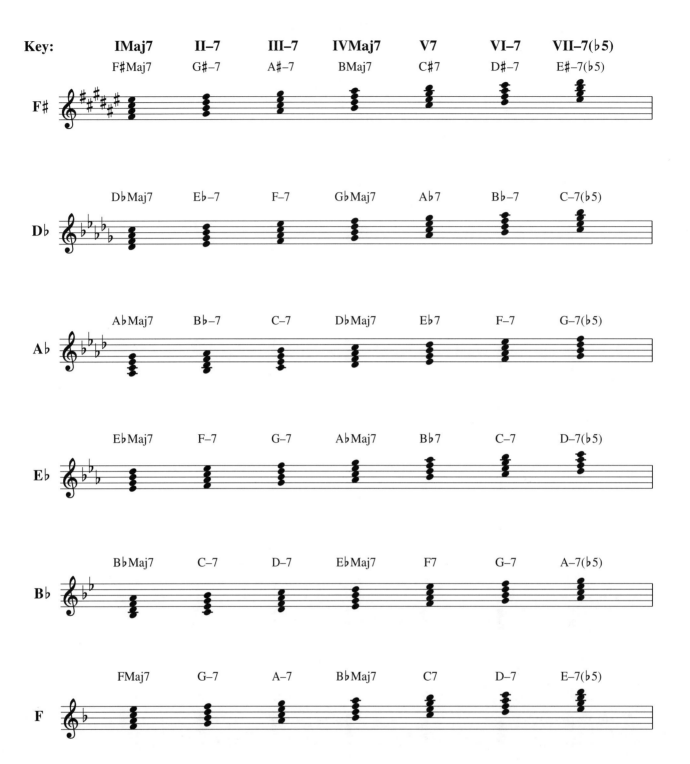

PART II

Rhythm and Expression

A great musical performance is much more than playing the right notes at the right time. Expression—dynamics and phrasing—is also a critical element that helps bring out the emotion in music. Once the scales, arpeggios, and exercises are under your fingers, practicing them within a more musical context will give you increased control of your instrument. The result will be more expressive performances.

It is helpful to first study rhythm, dynamics, and phrasing separately, then put them together, working towards combining *all* the musical elements in everything you play. Once you feel comfortable with each new skill, go back and incorporate it into your practice of scales, arpeggios, rhythmic groupings, and diatonic harmony. Listen to tracks 25–28 to hear examples; look for the track icons.

25–28

Control of Dynamics, Phrasing, and Articulation

Dynamics

There are infinite levels of dynamic gradations possible between the softest and loudest notes played on the piano. As pianists, the wider the volume range we are capable of playing, the more colorful and exciting our performance can be. The goal is to develop control so that you can play any passage of music as loudly or softly as appropriate to create the most musically expressive performance.

Start by practicing the scales, arpeggios, and exercises at your softest volume, keeping each note exactly the same dynamic as the last throughout the exercise. Then, experiment with how many volume ranges you can play consistently.

After getting a feel for a single dynamic, try changing the dynamics as you play the exercises. Make the changes gradual and smooth. Usually, performing music requires a balance of dynamics between the main theme (melody) and the secondary parts (harmony). Practice these dynamics at various tempos, remembering that fast and loud, or slow and soft, aren't always the best combinations.

Use only as much energy as needed to create the desired tone on the piano. Playing fortissimo does not require that every muscle of your body be tensed!

EXERCISES

Experiment with as many possible dynamic shadings as you can play while practicing the scales, arpeggios, exercises, and any musical passage you may be working on.

1. Ten dynamic ranges

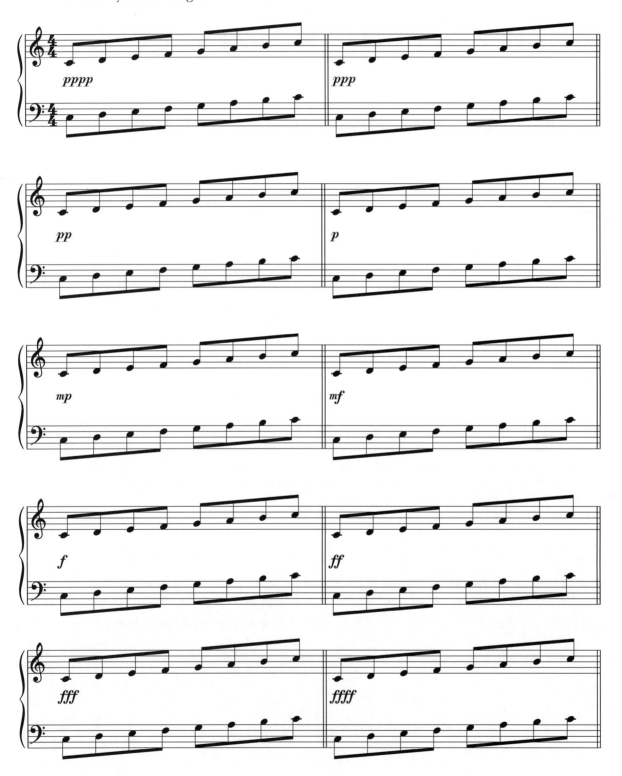

2. Dynamic gradations

These two-octave examples in C are only a starting point. Try them in all keys throughout the range of the piano. Also, experiment with your own dynamic shadings.

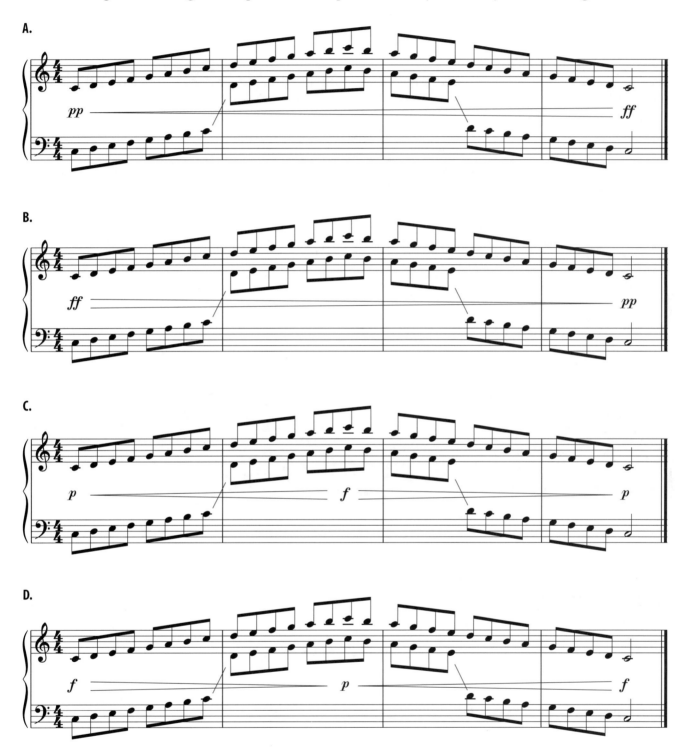

3. Two hands, two dynamics

A.

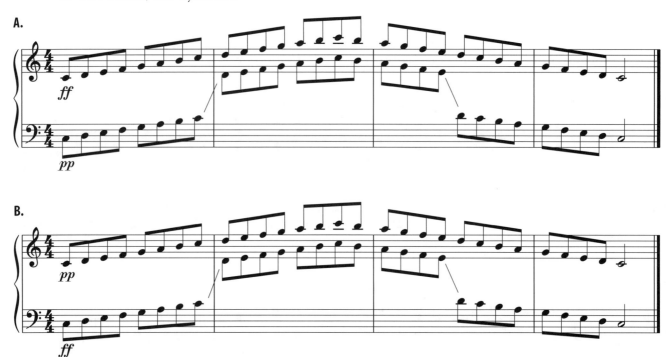

B.

4. Two hands, alternating dynamics

A.

B.

Articulation and Phrasing

The ability to control articulation and phrasing is critical to great performances. Incorporating articulation and phrasing in scale and arpeggio practice will greatly increase the musical value of these exercises, and will help build confidence in interpreting musical passages.

As with dynamics, there are infinite gradations of note detachment, so experiment with how short you choose to play notes that are marked staccato. Often the left hand and right hand will be notated to play different articulations, as in exercises 2 and 3. Exercises 1b and 1c combine phrases of varying length in the left and right hand, and the last exercise incorporates articulations with dynamic changes.

As you become comfortable with these elements, create your own phrases with dynamics, and watch for opportunities to apply both in the music you are studying.

Playing scales, arpeggios, and exercises staccato will probably be more physically taxing on your body, so practice staccato a little at a time until you become accustomed to these movements.

EXERCISES

1. Two-hand staccato and legato

A. Staccato

B. Staccato and Legato 1

C. Staccato and Legato 2

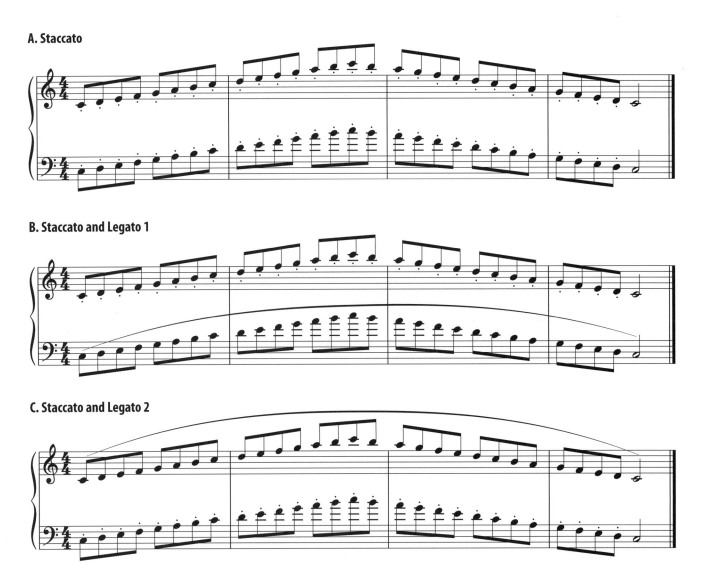

2. Mixed staccato and legato

27

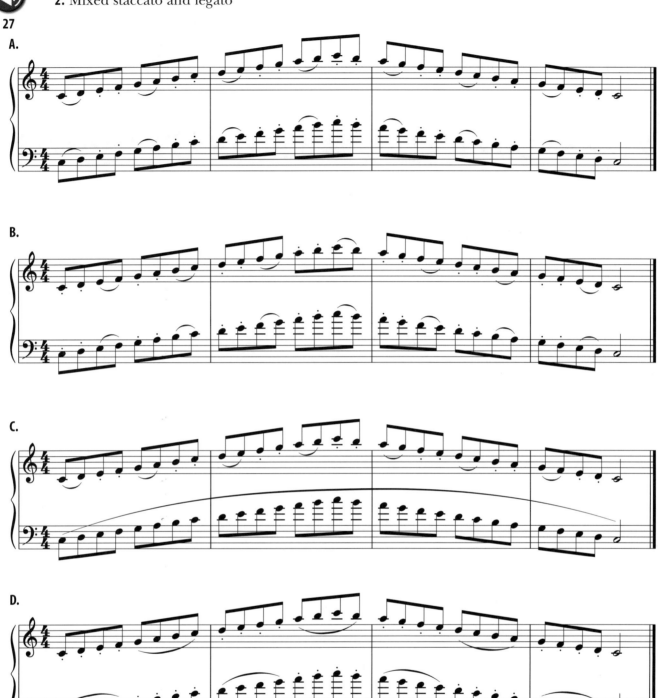

3. Combining phrasing and dynamics

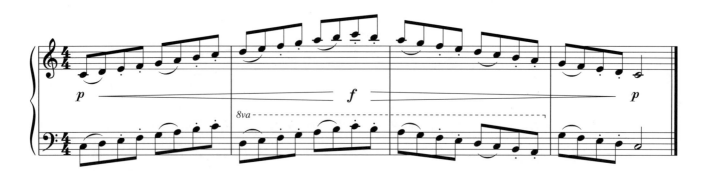

Continue to work on creating your own combinations of articulation, phrasing, dynamics, and rhythmic subdivisions. Track 26 is an example of staccato articulation using the C major scale with rhythmic subdivisions.

26

More Metronome Tips and Exploring Multiple Rhythms

The metronome can be used a number of ways to develop a sense of time. If you are having difficulty following the metronome, try doubling the tempo of the clicks, and think of the clicks as eighth notes rather than as quarter notes. If the song is composed of mostly eighth-note triplets, then triple the tempo setting to match those notes. The less time that goes by between clicks, the easier it is to follow the metronome. Conversely, if you can easily follow the metronome, try cutting the tempo setting in half, and thinking of the clicks as half notes. This is much more difficult to follow and is a great indicator of how steady your sense of tempo is.

Here are some examples with the metronome set at different values. The x mark indicates where the click should be.

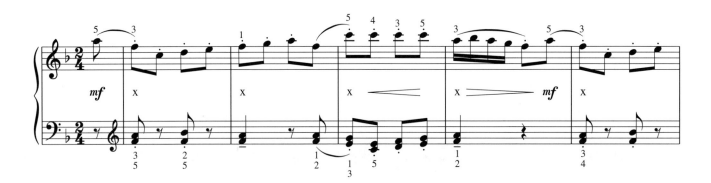

If you are studying music with jazz rhythms, set the metronome to click only on the second and fourth beats (the strong beats in this style of music).

30–33 Another fun way to practice is with a drum machine, or rhythm tracks from a computer, keyboard, or recording such as the one included with this book (tracks 30–33). Usually rhythm tracks are easier to follow, because the time is very clearly stated and subdivided. Pick rhythms that complement what you are working on. Don't try practicing swinging eighth notes over a drum machine that's playing a straight rock feel unless you are consciously trying to practice the contrast between the two styles. Listen to the demonstration on track 29, and rhythm tracks 30–33.

EXERCISES Rhythmic Variation

These rhythmic exercises will strengthen your sense of the subdivisions of each beat. Because notes don't always occur on the downbeat, it's important to be able to play any of the off-beats confidently. The tendency to drag or rush the time will also be greatly reduced. Practice these against a click or drum machine. It's helpful at first to use a metronome or drum pattern that will give you the subdivisions you are playing as well as the downbeats. Master each one before moving on to the next. Once you have mastered the given example, expand them to include all keys of scales and arpeggios throughout the range of the piano.

1.

2.   Sixteenth notes played off the beat may be thought of as staccato dotted eighth notes.

3.

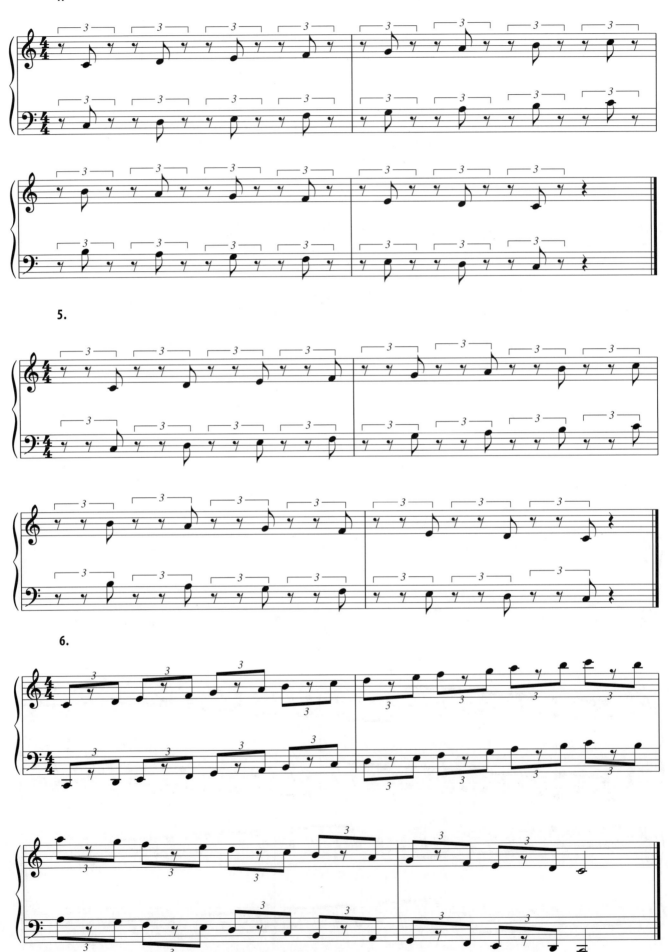

EXERCISES Rhythmic Contrast

The next exercises deal with playing two different rhythmic groupings at the same time with the left and right hands. I have included a number of common rhythmic groupings, but as with everything else, there are many possibilities. Explore some on your own, and don't forget to practice in all keys.

28

1.

2.

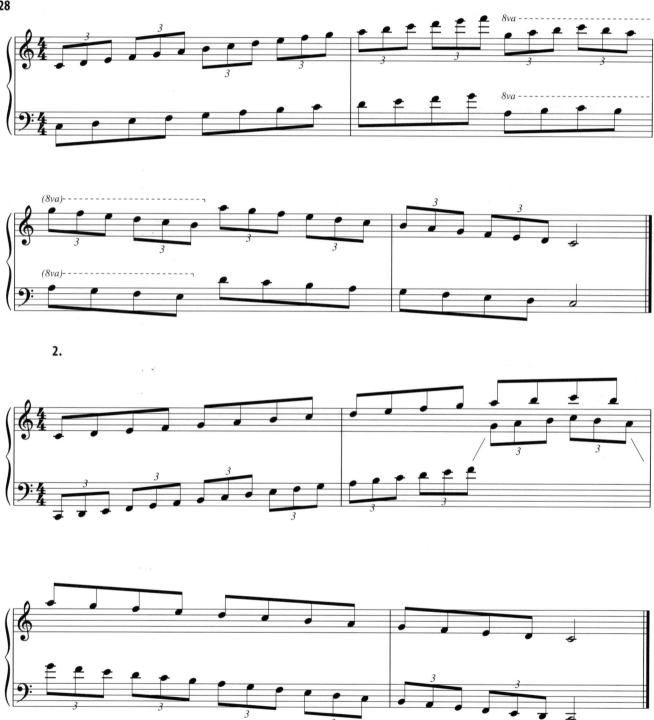

3.

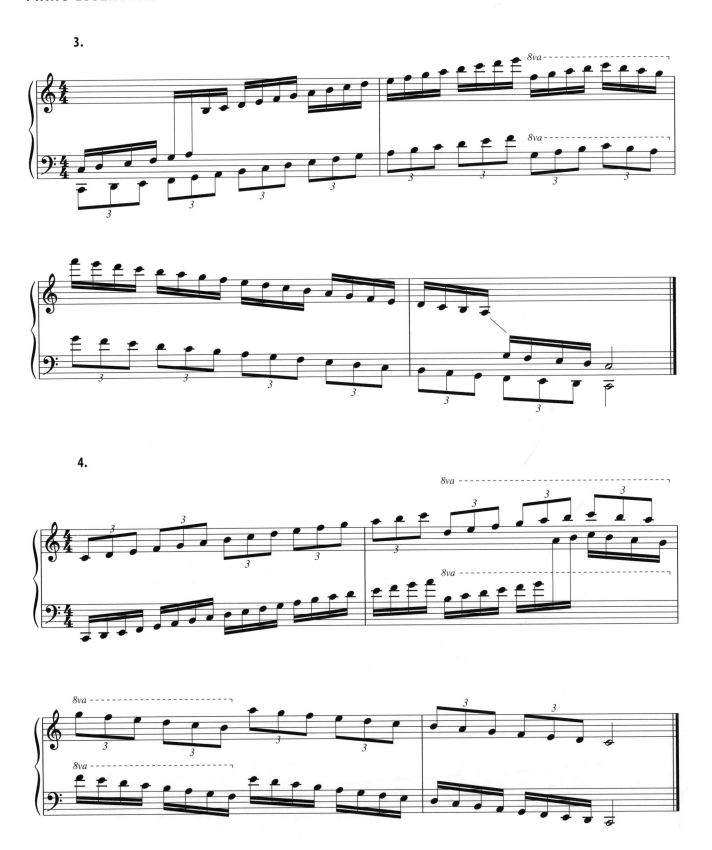

4.

PART III

Scale Studies in Minor Keys

To fully master minor keys as we have done with major, it is recommended that you learn all of the scales, arpeggios, and harmonic exercises in the book in minor, in all twelve keys. Part III is a text and reference for minor scales, to help bring you to your next level of development. The approach presented here will provide you with some structure in your ongoing growth as a musician.

Minor Scales

As you learned in chapter 1, there are many possible combinations of whole steps and half steps, forming numerous scales and related harmony. Minor scales can be found in all styles of music, and are equally important to master.

Always try to see and hear the scales and patterns in the songs you are working on. To get the most out of this section, practice all forms of the minor scales, and apply all of the arpeggios and exercises in the major key section to melodic and harmonic minor keys.

The natural minor scale (also known as relative minor, pure minor, and Aeolian mode) is most easily found by playing any major scale using its sixth scale degree as a start and end point.

C Major, Two Octaves

A Natural-Minor

Each major key has one relative minor scale associated with it. Both scales share the same key signature. For example, both C major and A minor have no sharps and no flats, while G major and E minor both have one sharp.

Another way of arriving at the natural minor scale is to follow its scale formula. The whole step/half step formula for the natural minor scale is as follows:

A Minor, Two Octaves

There are three commonly used variations of the natural minor: harmonic minor, traditional melodic minor, and jazz melodic minor.

Harmonic minor: contains a raised seventh scale degree from natural minor.

Traditional melodic minor: the sixth and seventh scale degrees are raised ascending, and lowered descending.

Jazz melodic minor: the sixth and seventh scale degrees are raised both ascending and descending. Jazz melodic minor, also known as "real" melodic minor, may be easier to think of as simply a major scale with a flatted third scale degree.

Mastering Minor Keys

To master minor keys, first learn harmonic minor scales and arpeggios. Learn them thoroughly before moving to the other forms. The transition to traditional and jazz melodic is much easier once you're comfortable with harmonic minor. The diatonic triad arpeggios are the same, regardless of what minor scale you are using, because they all share a minor third and perfect fifth.

As with the exercises in major, try to see and hear these scales and patterns in the songs you are working with. Improvisers and composers will find a vast supply of both harmonic and melodic ideas after studying these scales and their harmony.

Harmonic Minor Scales and Arpeggios

A Harmonic Minor

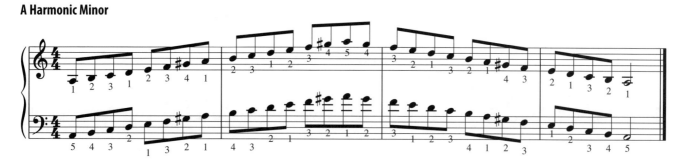

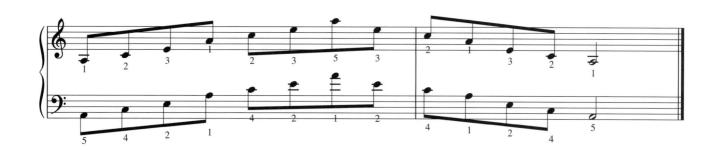

E Harmonic Minor

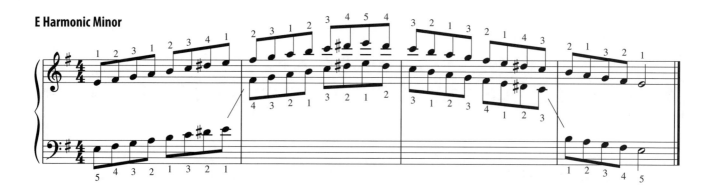

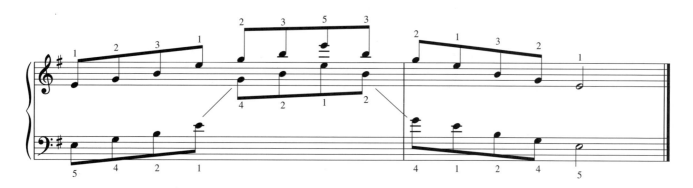

B Harmonic Minor

F# Harmonic Minor

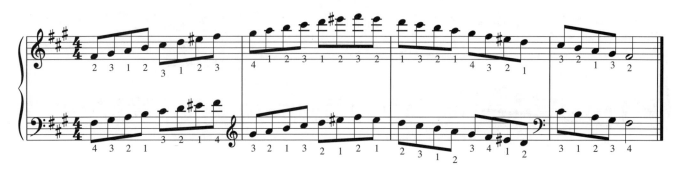

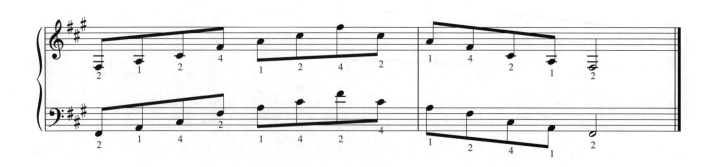

C♯ Harmonic Minor

G♯ Harmonic Minor

E♭ Harmonic Minor

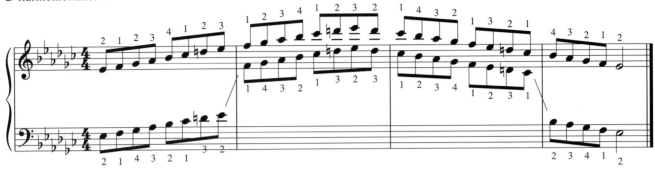

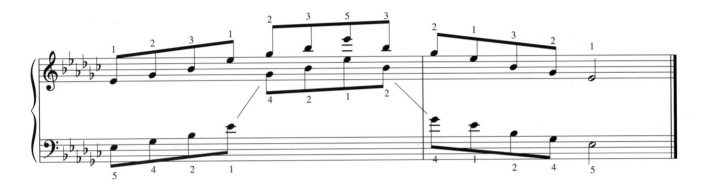

B♭ Harmonic Minor

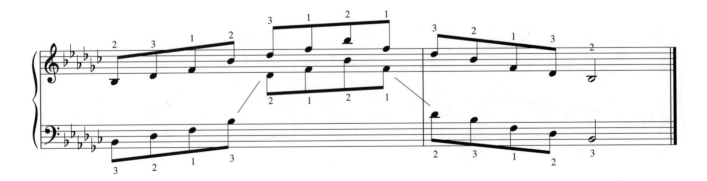

F Harmonic Minor

C Harmonic Minor

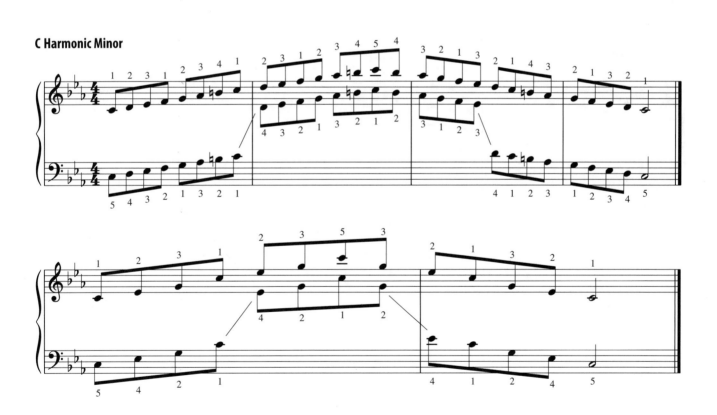

PIANO ESSENTIALS

G Harmonic Minor

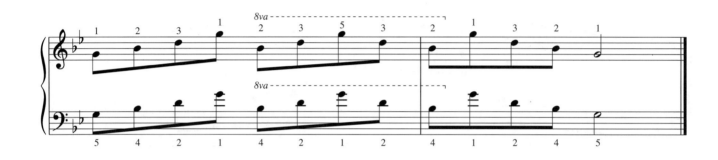

D Harmonic Minor

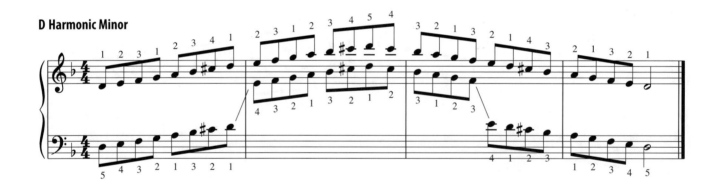

Harmonic Minor Diatonic Seventh Chord Qualities

Here are diatonic seventh chords in the key of C harmonic minor. Remember, the diatonic chord *qualities* (major, minor, etc.) are identical regardless of key.

Diatonic Seventh Chord Construction Based on C Harmonic Minor Scale:

Harmonic Minor Diatonic Seventh Chords, Twelve Keys

Traditional Melodic Minor Scales

A Traditional Melodic Minor

E Traditional Melodic Minor

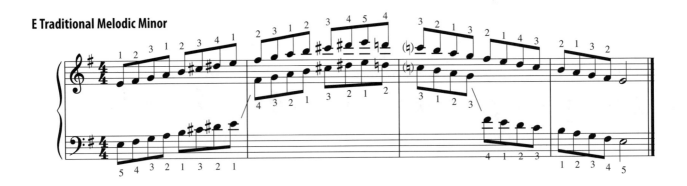

B Traditional Melodic Minor

F♯ Traditional Melodic Minor

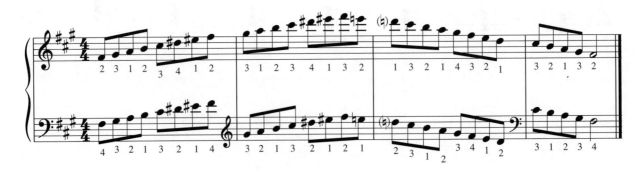

C♯ Traditional Melodic Minor

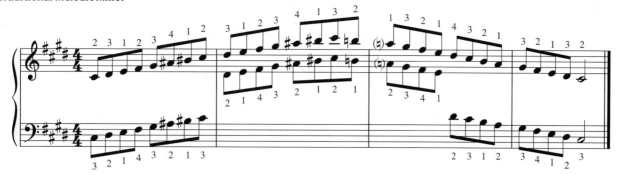

G♯ Traditional Melodic Minor

E♭ Traditional Melodic Minor

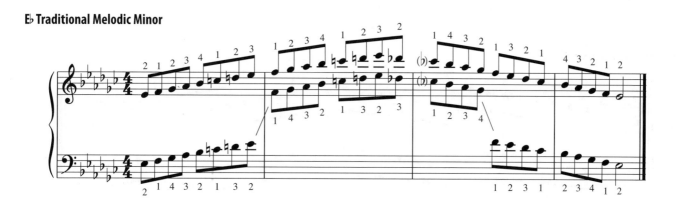

B♭ Traditional Melodic Minor

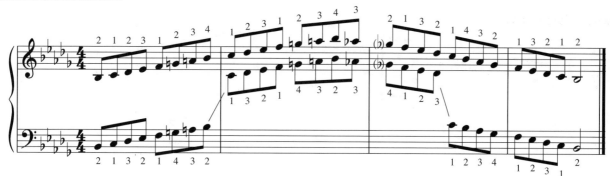

F Traditional Melodic Minor

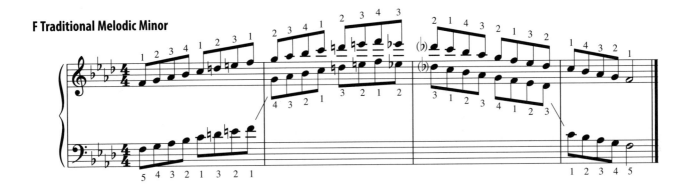

C Traditional Melodic Minor

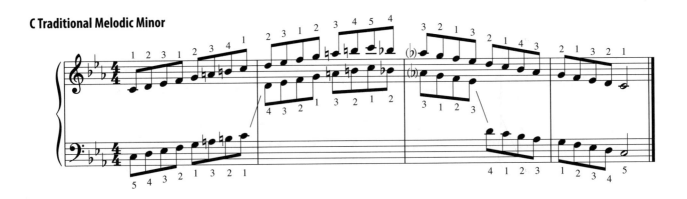

G Traditional Melodic Minor

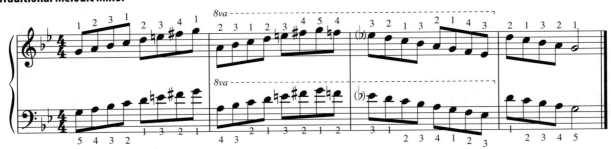

D Traditional Melodic Minor

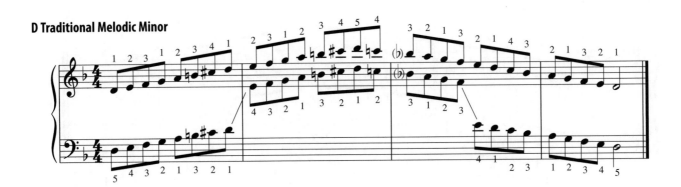

Jazz (Real) Melodic Minor Scales

A Jazz Melodic Minor

E Jazz Melodic Minor

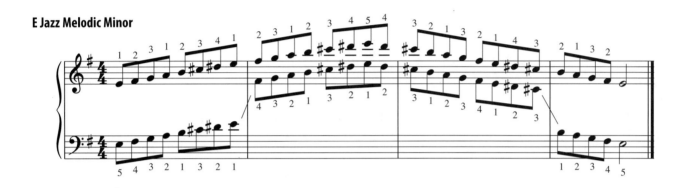

B Jazz Melodic Minor

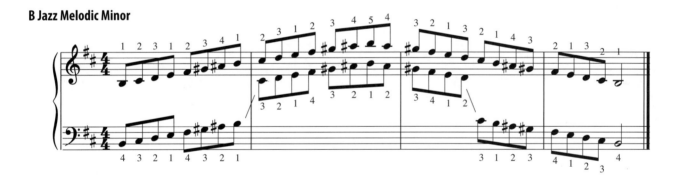

F# Jazz Melodic Minor

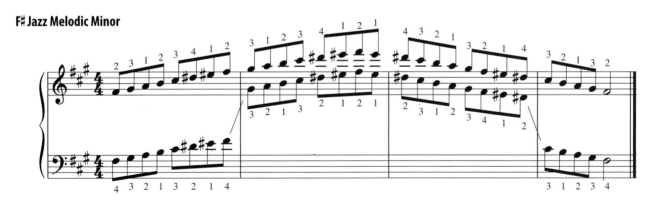

C♯ Jazz Melodic Minor

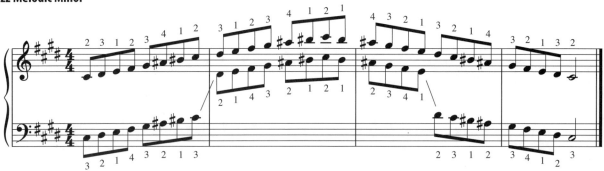

G♯ Jazz Melodic Minor

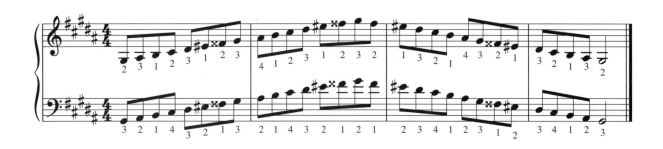

E♭ Jazz Melodic Minor

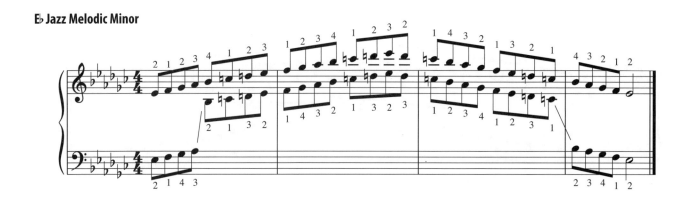

B♭ Jazz Melodic Minor

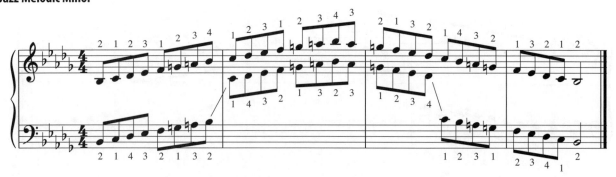

F Jazz Melodic Minor

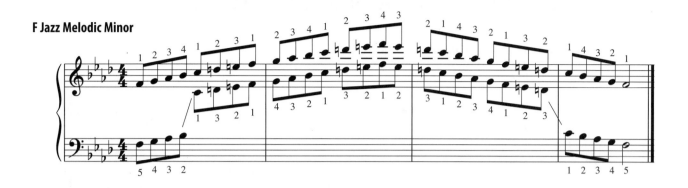

C Jazz Melodic Minor

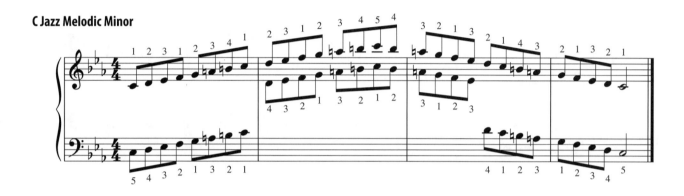

G Jazz Melodic Minor

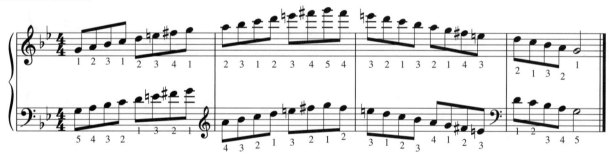

D Jazz Melodic Minor

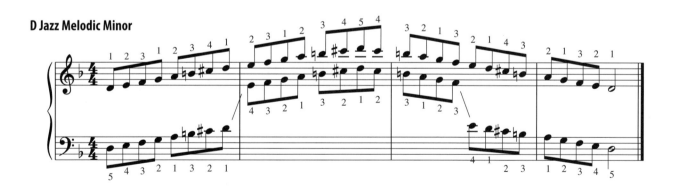

Jazz Melodic Minor Diatonic Seventh Chord Qualities

Diatonic Seventh Chord Construction Based on C Jazz Melodic Minor Scale:

Jazz Melodic Minor Diatonic Seventh Chords, Twelve Keys

Additional Cadences for Minor Keys

Minor cadences 1 and 2 below are required of second-semester Berklee students. These first two common minor cadences are built around harmonic minor harmony. Notice that the II chord in cadence 2 is played with the third of the chord in the root. In classical music, this chord inversion is notated as a $\frac{6}{3}$ chord. In more modern music, it is commonly notated as a "slash" chord, such as D°/F.

The challenge cadence is a Level 3 cadence requirement, and is a common progression of chords. It moves up by fourths (or down by fifths) to cycle through all diatonic seventh chords in major key harmony. You can also substitute minor diatonic chords into the third progression. Countless songs are built around this type of progression.

Cadence 1.

Practice this I– IV– V cadence in all keys, starting first in root position, then starting in first inversion, then starting in second inversion.

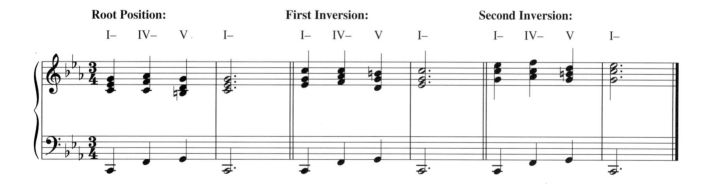

Cadence 2.

Practice this cadence in all keys, starting in root position, then in first inversion, then second inversion.

CHALLENGE   Cadence 3.

This advanced cadence draws on all that you have learned about harmony and voice leading up to this point. It starts with the I chord in third inversion. Practice it in all keys. Notice that the roots of the chords are omitted from the right-hand voicing and played only with the left hand.

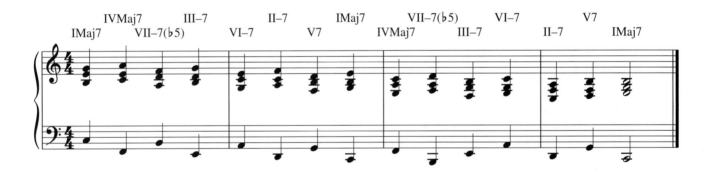

PART IV

More Key-Area Studies

At this point, you should have mastered the major and minor scales that are part of the Berklee College of Music Piano Department Level I and II requirements. Part IV presents more advanced concepts that you may find helpful in further developing your technique.

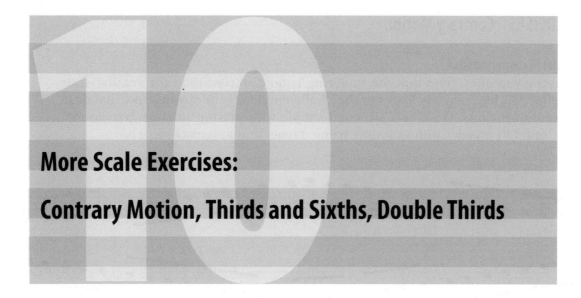

More Scale Exercises:

Contrary Motion, Thirds and Sixths, Double Thirds

In many styles of piano music, it is not uncommon to find scales played in intervals of thirds, sixths, or moving in contrary motion. Studying these variations will prepare you for those challenges. Practice each variation, one key at a time, remembering that accurate performance only comes from accurate practice. These reference pages are a very large undertaking and may be incorporated into your playing over years of study. You will get the best results by being organized and deliberate, mastering one variation, one key at a time. After you are comfortable with fingerings, remember to apply various dynamics, articulations, and when possible, contrasting rhythms.

Practice these exercises in one, two, three, and four octaves, in four rhythmic groupings, as you did in chapter 4, pages 34–36. Note that the physical range of the piano limits you to three octaves in contrary motion.

NOTE: The fingerings for thirds and sixths I chose for clarity. In some instances, it may be easier to start with fingers other than as notated. For example, on the C major scale in thirds, the second finger can also be used to start the right hand. Feel free to adjust to your fingering preference.

EXERCISES Contrary Motion

1. Scales in contrary motion

In contrary motion, note that the fingering is no different than the regular scale fingering you have already learned; the challenge here is in moving your hands in opposite directions. Once you are comfortable with playing in contrary motion, don't forget to practice with various dynamic ranges and articulations.

2. Arpeggios in contrary motion

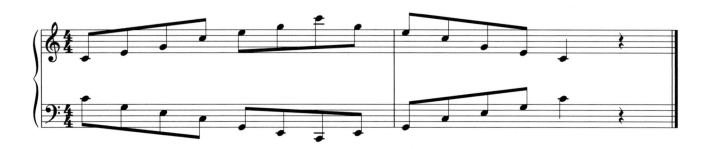

EXERCISES Thirds and Sixths

1. Major scales in thirds and sixths, two octaves, twelve keys

The first line of music in each key is in thirds; the second is in sixths. These scales are part of the Berklee Piano Department Level 5 technique requirements. Play in four octaves, with four rhythmic groupings, as shown on pages 34–36.

C Major

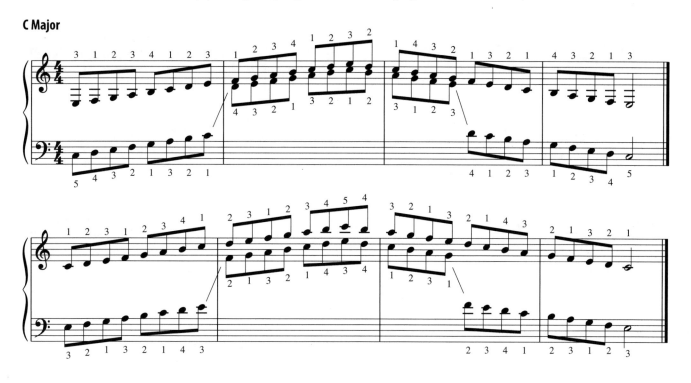

G Major

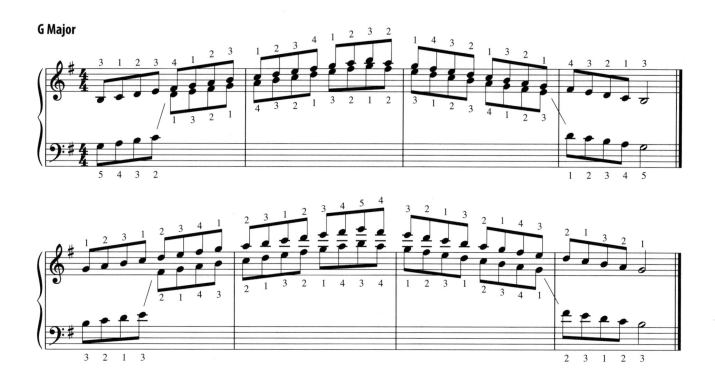

D Major

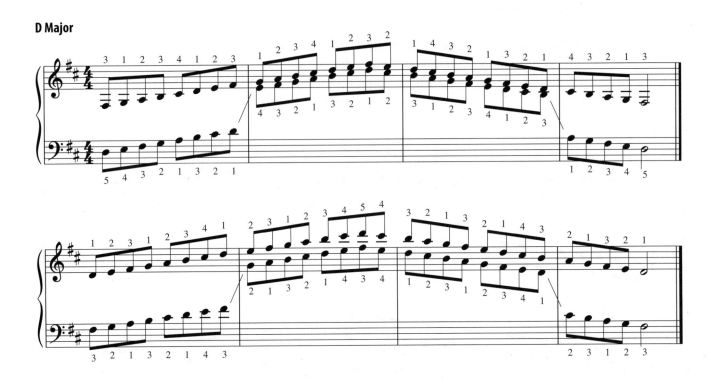

A Major

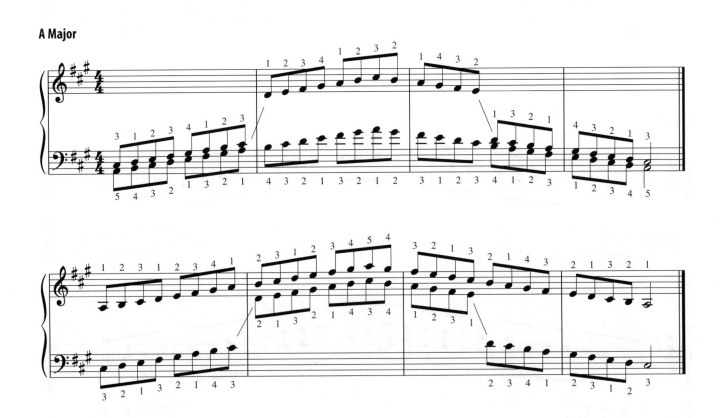

E Major

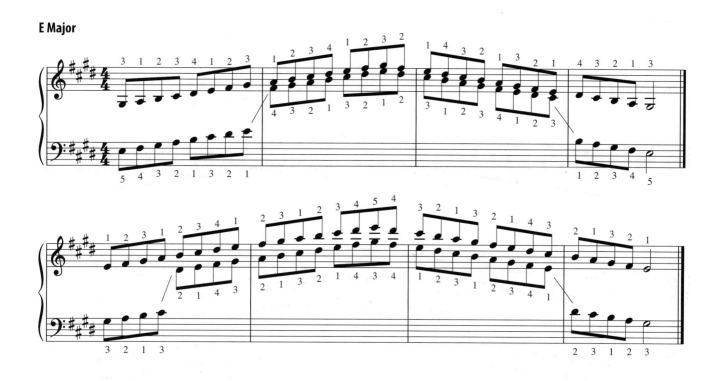

B Major

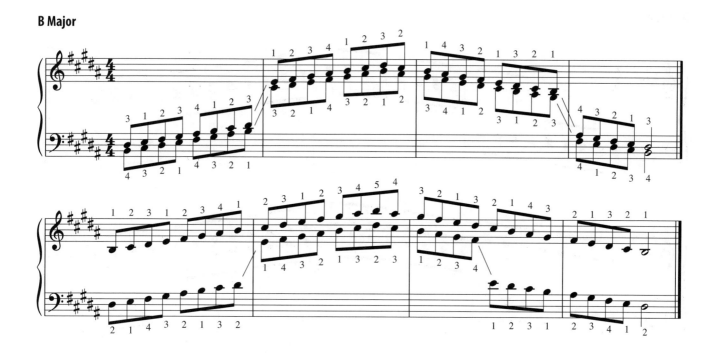

G♭ Major

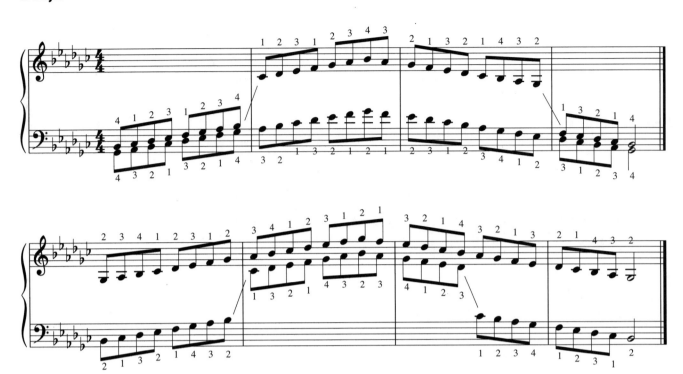

D♭ Major

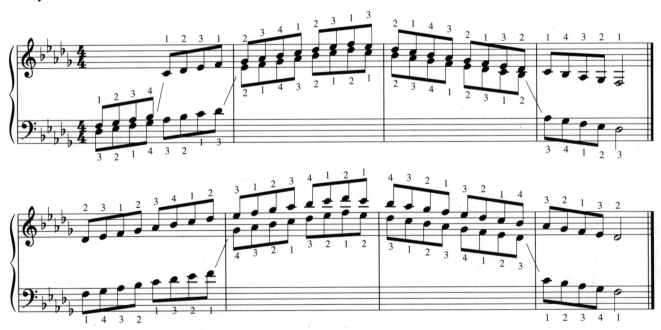

A♭ Major

E♭ Major

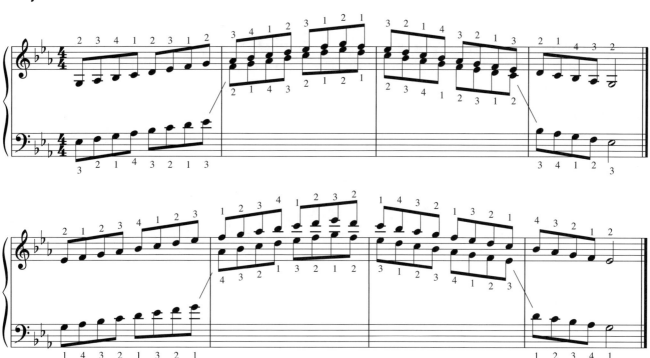

Bb Major

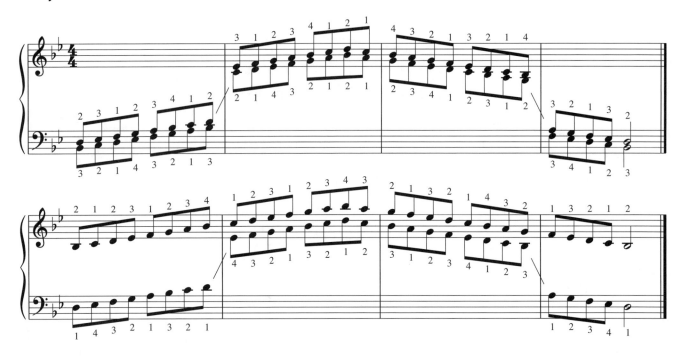

F Major

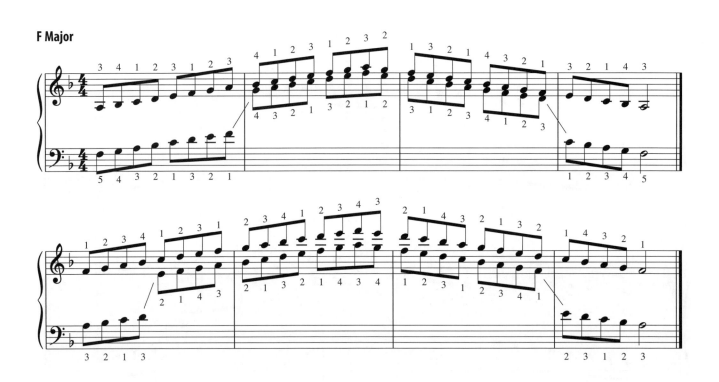

2. Harmonic minor scales in thirds and sixths, two octaves, twelve keys

As before, the first line of music in each key is in thirds, the second is in sixths. These scales are part of the Berklee Piano Department Level 6 technique requirements, in four octaves, with four rhythmic groupings, as shown on pages 34–36.

A Harmonic Minor

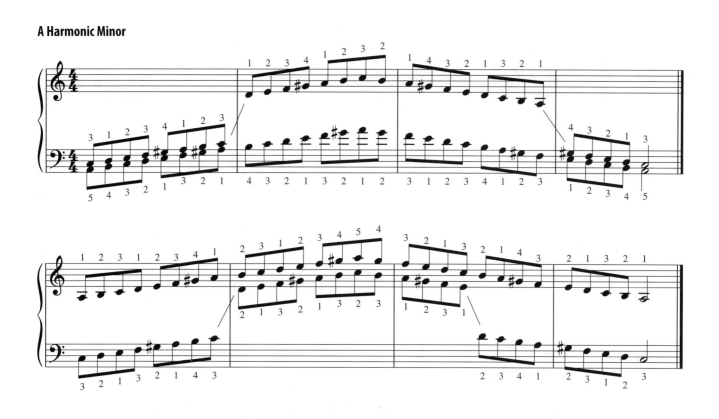

E Harmonic Minor

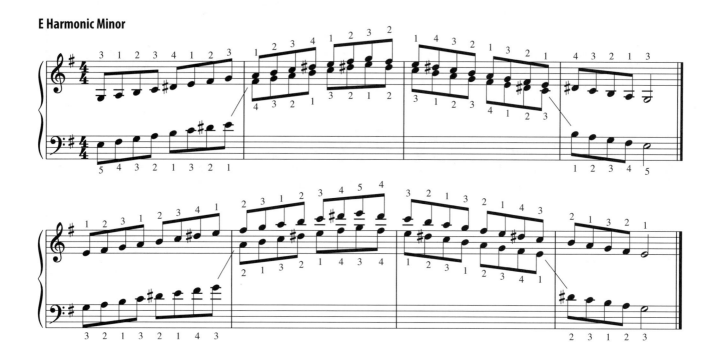

B Harmonic Minor

F♯ Harmonic Minor

C♯ Harmonic Minor

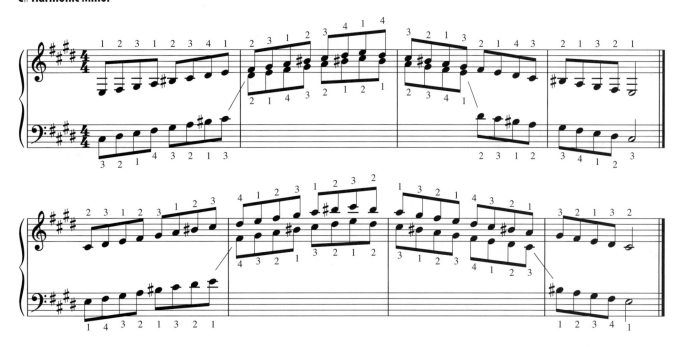

G♯ Harmonic Minor

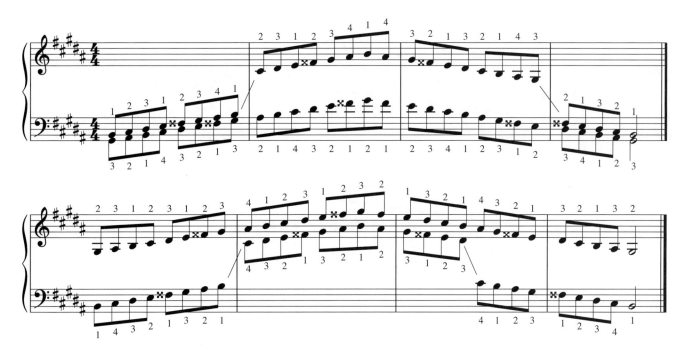

E♭ Harmonic Minor

B♭ Harmonic Minor

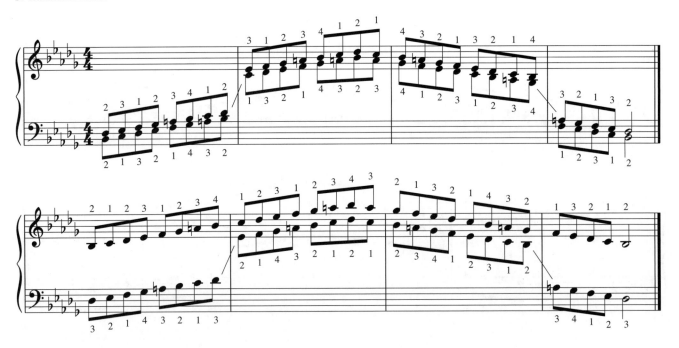

F Harmonic Minor

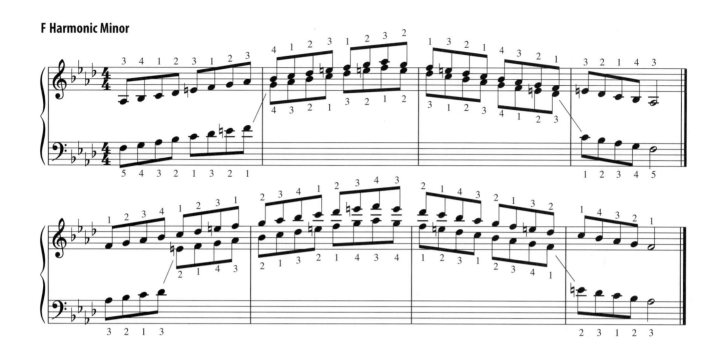

C Harmonic Minor

G Harmonic Minor

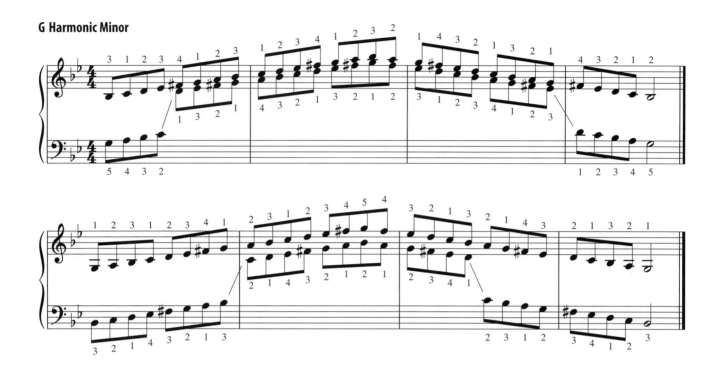

D Harmonic Minor

EXERCISES Double Thirds

Scales in double thirds for major and minor

The highly motivated student can also work on scales in double thirds. This will further strengthen technique. Double thirds are often used as a way of harmonizing melodic lines and function well in all styles of music.

A single fingering will not work for all keys. The chart on the following page shows you the appropriate fingering for each key. Here is the fingering from the chart, applied to the key of C, in one octave. Work towards being able to play it in one, two, three, and four octaves.

C Major

C Major
RH: 3 4 5 2 3 4 5
    1 2 3 1 1 2 3
LH: 3 2 1 3 2 1 1
    5 4 3 5 4 3 2

G Major
RH: 3 4 5 2 3 4 5
    1 2 3 1 1 2 3
LH: 3 2 1 3 2 1 1
    5 4 3 5 4 3 2

D Major
RH: 3 4 5 2 3 4 5
    1 2 3 1 1 2 3
LH: 3 2 1 3 2 1 1
    5 4 3 5 4 3 2

A Major
RH: 3 4 5 2 3 4 5
    1 2 3 1 1 2 3
LH: 3 2 1 3 2 1 1
    5 4 3 5 4 3 2

E Major
RH: 3 4 5 2 3 4 5
    1 2 3 1 1 2 3
LH: 3 2 1 3 2 1 1
    5 4 3 5 4 3 2

B Major
RH: 3 4 5 2 3 4 5
    1 2 3 1 1 2 3
LH: 2 1 3 2 1 1 3
    4 3 5 4 3 2 5

G♭ Major
RH: 3 4 5 3 4 5 2
    1 2 3 1 2 3 1
LH: 1 1 3 2 1 3 2
    3 2 5 4 3 5 4

D♭ Major
RH: 4 5 2 3 4 5 3
    2 3 1 1 2 3 1
LH: 1 3 2 1 1 3 2
    3 5 4 3 2 5 4

A♭ Major
RH: 4 5 3 4 5 2 3
    2 3 1 2 3 1 1
LH: 1 3 2 1 1 3 2
    3 5 4 3 2 5 4

E♭ Major
RH: 5 2 3 4 5 3 4
    3 1 1 2 3 1 2
LH: 1 3 2 1 1 3 2
    3 5 4 3 2 5 4

B♭ Major
RH: 5 2 3 4 5 3 4
    3 1 1 2 3 1 2
LH: 1 3 2 1 1 3 2
    3 5 4 3 2 5 4

F Major
RH: 2 3 4 5 3 4 5
    1 1 2 3 1 2 3
LH: 3 2 1 1 3 2 1
    5 4 3 2 5 4 3

C Harmonic Minor
RH: 3 4 5 2 3 4 5
    1 2 3 1 1 2 3
LH: 3 2 1 3 2 1 1
    5 4 3 5 4 3 2

G Harmonic Minor
RH: 3 4 5 2 3 4 5
    1 2 3 1 1 2 3
LH: 3 2 1 3 2 1 1
    5 4 3 5 4 3 2

D Harmonic Minor
RH: 3 4 5 2 3 4 5
    1 2 3 1 1 2 3
LH: 3 2 1 3 2 1 1
    5 4 3 5 4 3 2

A Harmonic Minor
RH: 3 4 5 2 3 4 5
    1 2 3 1 1 2 3
LH: 3 2 1 3 2 1 1
    5 4 3 5 4 3 2

E Harmonic Minor
RH: 3 4 5 2 3 4 5
    1 2 3 1 1 2 3
LH: 2 1 1 3 2 1 3
    4 3 2 5 4 3 5

B Harmonic Minor
RH: 4 5 2 3 4 5 3
    2 3 1 1 2 3 1
LH: 2 1 3 2 1 1 3
    4 3 5 4 3 2 5

F♯ Harmonic Minor
RH: 4 5 3 4 5 2 3
    2 3 1 2 3 1 1
LH: 1 1 3 2 1 3 2
    3 2 5 4 3 5 4

D♭ Harmonic Minor
RH: 4 5 3 4 5 2 3
    2 3 1 2 3 1 1
LH: 1 3 2 1 1 3 2
    3 5 4 3 2 5 4

A♭ Harmonic Minor
RH: 4 5 3 4 5 2 3
    2 3 1 2 3 1 1
LH: 1 3 2 1 1 3 2
    3 5 4 3 2 5 4

E♭ Harmonic Minor
RH: 5 2 3 4 5 3 4
    3 1 1 2 3 1 2
LH: 1 3 2 1 1 3 2
    3 5 4 3 2 5 4

B♭ Harmonic Minor
RH: 5 3 4 5 2 3 4
    3 1 2 3 1 1 2
LH: 3 2 1 3 2 1 1
    5 4 3 5 4 3 2

F Harmonic Minor
RH: 2 3 4 5 3 4 5
    1 1 2 3 1 2 3
LH: 3 2 1 3 2 1 1
    5 4 3 5 4 3 2

Conclusion

In this book, you have learned major and minor scales and arpeggios and have gained a fundamental understanding of the theory behind these scales and the harmony built from them. You have completed the technique requirements for a first and second semester Berklee piano student. Through practicing the scales, chords, arpeggios, and cadences, you have improved your tone, dynamic range, and sense of rhythm. You have more musical phrasing, more comfort with fingerings, and have increased speed and agility on the keyboard.

As you continue to grow as a musician, remember that *you* are your own best teacher. Once you feel comfortable with the information and techniques you have learned here, find ways to use this knowledge to create your own music. These essential elements will hopefully give you the tools to help express it. Enjoy the process of learning because if you are fortunate, it will never end.

About the Author

Ross Ramsay, faculty in the Piano Department at Berklee College of Music, has been teaching piano for twenty-five years, and has been included in the Who's Who List of American Teachers several times. He composes and produces music for local and nationally broadcast television, radio, cable, and video programs, and has been a featured soloist on piano and keyboards with various artists touring throughout the United States and Europe. Ross is a product specialist and clinician for Yamaha Corporation of America, Digital Musical Instruments and Pro Audio Division. He received a Bachelor of Music from Berklee College of Music in 1986.

For more information, please visit his website at www.RossRamsay.com

More Fine Publications

Berklee Press

GUITAR

BEBOP GUITAR SOLOS
by Michael Kaplan
00121703 Book $16.99

BLUES GUITAR TECHNIQUE
by Michael Williams
50449623 Book/Online Audio..........$24.99

BERKLEE GUITAR CHORD DICTIONARY
by Rick Peckham
50449546 Jazz - Book........................$12.99
50449596 Rock - Book........................$12.99

BERKLEE GUITAR STYLE STUDIES
by Jim Kelly
00200377 Book/Online Media..........$24.99

CLASSICAL TECHNIQUE FOR THE MODERN GUITARIST
by Kim Perlak
00148781 Book/Online Audio..............$19.99

CONTEMPORARY JAZZ GUITAR SOLOS
by Michael Kaplan
00143596 ....$16.99

CREATIVE CHORDAL HARMONY FOR GUITAR
by Mick Goodrick and Tim Miller
50449613 Book/Online Audio..............$19.99

FUNK/R&B GUITAR
by Thaddeus Hogarth
50449569 Book/Online Audio $19.99

GUITAR CHOP SHOP – BUILDING ROCK/METAL TECHNIQUE
by Joe Stump
50449601 Book/Online Audio $19.99

GUITAR SWEEP PICKING
by Joe Stump
00151223 Book/Online Audio..............$19.99

INTRODUCTION TO JAZZ GUITAR
by Jane Miller
00125041 Book/Online Audio $19.99

JAZZ GUITAR FRETBOARD NAVIGATION
by Mark White
00154107 Book/Online Audio $19.99

JAZZ SWING GUITAR
by Jon Wheatley
00139935 Book/Online Audio..............$19.99

A MODERN METHOD FOR GUITAR*
by William Leavitt
Volume 1: Beginner
00137387 Book/Online Video $24.99
*Other volumes, media options, and supporting songbooks available.

A MODERN METHOD FOR GUITAR SCALES
by Larry Baione
00199318 Book...$10.99

Berklee Press publications feature material developed at the Berklee College of Music.
To browse the complete Berklee Press Catalog, go to
www.berkleepress.com

BASS

BASS LINES
Fingerstyle Funk
by Joe Santerre
50449542 Book/Online Audio $19.95
Metal
by David Marvuglio
00122465 Book/Online Audio.............$19.99
Rock
by Joe Santerre
50449478 Book/CD $19.95

BERKLEE JAZZ BASS
by Rich Appleman, Whit Browne, and Bruce Gertz
50449636 Book/Online Audio $19.99

FUNK BASS FILLS
by Anthony Vitti
50449608 Book/Online Audio...........$19.99

INSTANT BASS
by Danny Morris
50449502 Book/CD $9.99

VOICE

BELTING
by Jeannie Gagné
00124984 Book/Online Media $19.99

THE CONTEMPORARY SINGER – 2ND ED.
by Anne Peckham
50449595 Book/Online Audio $24.99

JAZZ VOCAL IMPROVISATION
by Mili Bermejo
00159290 Book/Online Audio $19.99

TIPS FOR SINGERS
by Carolyn Wilkins
50449557 Book/CD $19.95

VOCAL TECHNIQUE
featuring Anne Peckham
50448038 DVD.......................................$19.95

VOCAL WORKOUTS FOR THE CONTEMPORARY SINGER
by Anne Peckham
50448044 Book/Online Audio..........$24.99

YOUR SINGING VOICE
by Jeannie Gagné
50449619 Book/Online Audio $29.99

WOODWINDS/BRASS

TRUMPET SOUND EFFECTS
by Craig Pederson & Ueli Dörig
00121626 Book/Online Audio.............$14.99

SAXOPHONE SOUND EFFECTS
by Ueli Dörig
50449628 Book/Online Audio $15.99

THE TECHNIQUE OF THE FLUTE: CHORD STUDIES, RHYTHM STUDIES
by Joseph Viola
00214012 Book.......................................$19.99

PIANO/KEYBOARD

BERKLEE JAZZ KEYBOARD HARMONY
by Suzanna Sifter
00138874 Book/Online Audio...........$24.99

BERKLEE JAZZ PIANO
by Ray Santisi
50448047 Book/Online Audio $19.99

BERKLEE JAZZ STANDARDS FOR SOLO PIANO
Arranged by Robert Christopherson, Hey Rim Jeon, Ross Ramsay, Tim Ray
00160482 Book/Online Audio...........$19.99

CHORD-SCALE IMPROVISATION FOR KEYBOARD
by Ross Ramsay
50449597 Book/CD................................$19.99

CONTEMPORARY PIANO TECHNIQUE
by Stephany Tiernan
50449545 Book/DVD $29.99

HAMMOND ORGAN COMPLETE
by Dave Limina
50449479 Book/CD $24.99

JAZZ PIANO COMPING
by Suzanne Davis
50449614 Book/Online Audio $19.99

LATIN JAZZ PIANO IMPROVISATION
by Rebecca Cline
50449649 Book/Online Audio..........$24.99

SOLO JAZZ PIANO – 2ND ED.
by Neil Olmstead
50449641 Book/Online Audio...........$39.99

DRUMS

BEGINNING DJEMBE
by Michael Markus & Joe Galeota
00148210 Book/Online Video $16.99

BERKLEE JAZZ DRUMS
by Casey Scheuerell
50449612 Book/Online Audio...........$19.99

DRUM SET WARM-UPS
by Rod Morgenstein
50449465 Book.......................................$12.99

A MANUAL FOR THE MODERN DRUMMER
by Alan Dawson & Don DeMichael
50449560 Book.......................................$14.99

MASTERING THE ART OF BRUSHES – 2ND EDITION
by Jon Hazilla
50449459 Book/Online Audio $19.99

PHRASING: ADVANCED RUDIMENTS FOR CREATIVE DRUMMING
by Russ Gold
00120209 Book/Online Media............$19.99

WORLD JAZZ DRUMMING
by Mark Walker
50449568 Book/CD $22.99

STRINGS/ROOTS MUSIC

BERKLEE HARP
Chords, Styles, and Improvisation for Pedal and Lever Harp
by Felice Pomeranz
00144263 Book/Online Audio $19.99

BEYOND BLUEGRASS
Beyond Bluegrass Banjo
by Dave Hollander and Matt Glaser
50449610 Book/CD $19.99

Beyond Bluegrass Mandolin
by John McGann and Matt Glaser
50449609 Book/CD $19.99

Bluegrass Fiddle and Beyond
by Matt Glaser
50449602 Book/CD $19.99

EXPLORING CLASSICAL MANDOLIN
by August Watters
00125040 Book/Online Media $19.99

THE IRISH CELLO BOOK
by Liz Davis Maxfield
50449652 Book/Online Audio $24.99

JAZZ UKULELE
by Abe Lagrimas, Jr.
00121624 Book/Online Audio $19.99

BERKLEE PRACTICE METHOD

GET YOUR BAND TOGETHER
With additional volumes for other instruments, plus a teacher's guide.
Bass
by Rich Appleman, John Repucci and the Berklee Faculty
50449427 Book/CD $16.99
Drum Set
by Ron Savage, Casey Scheuerell and the Berklee Faculty
50449429 Book/CD $14.95
Guitar
by Larry Baione and the Berklee Faculty
50449426 Book/CD $16.99
Keyboard
by Russell Hoffmann, Paul Schmeling and the Berklee Faculty
50449428 Book/Online Audio $14.99

WELLNESS

MANAGE YOUR STRESS AND PAIN THROUGH MUSIC
by Dr. Suzanne B. Hanser and Dr. Susan E. Mandel
50449592 Book/CD $29.99

MUSICIAN'S YOGA
by Mia Olson
50449587 Book $17.99

THE NEW MUSIC THERAPIST'S HANDBOOK – 3RD EDITION
by Dr. Suzanne B. Hanser
00279325 Book $29.99

AUTOBIOGRAPHY

LEARNING TO LISTEN: THE JAZZ JOURNEY OF GARY BURTON
by Gary Burton
00117798 Book $27.99

HAL•LEONARD®

Prices subject to change without notice. Visit your local music dealer or bookstore, or go to **www.berkleepress.com**

MUSIC THEORY/EAR TRAINING/ IMPROVISATION

BEGINNING EAR TRAINING
by Gilson Schachnik
50449548 Book/Online Audio $16.99

THE BERKLEE BOOK OF JAZZ HARMONY
by Joe Mulholland & Tom Hojnacki
00113755 Book/Online Audio $27.50

BERKLEE MUSIC THEORY – 2ND ED.
by Paul Schmeling
Rhythm, Scales Intervals
50449615 Book/Online Audio $24.99
Harmony
50449616 Book/Online Audio $22.99

IMPROVISATION FOR CLASSICAL MUSICIANS
by Eugene Friesen with Wendy M. Friesen
50449637 Book/CD $24.99

REHARMONIZATION TECHNIQUES
by Randy Felts
50449496 Book $29.99

MUSIC BUSINESS

ENGAGING THE CONCERT AUDIENCE
by David Wallace
00244532 Book/Online Media $16.99

HOW TO GET A JOB IN THE MUSIC INDUSTRY – 3RD EDITION
by Keith Hatschek with Breanne Beseda
00130699 Book $27.99

MAKING MUSIC MAKE MONEY
by Eric Beall
50448009 Book $27.99

MUSIC LAW IN THE DIGITAL AGE – 2ND EDITION
by Allen Bargfrede
00148196 Book $19.99

MUSIC MARKETING
by Mike King
50449588 Book $24.99

PROJECT MANAGEMENT FOR MUSICIANS
by Jonathan Feist
50449659 Book $27.99

THE SELF-PROMOTING MUSICIAN – 3RD EDITION
by Peter Spellman
00119607 Book $24.99

MUSIC PRODUCTION & ENGINEERING

AUDIO MASTERING
by Jonathan Wyner
50449581 Book/CD $29.99

AUDIO POST PRODUCTION
by Mark Cross
50449627 Book $19.99

THE SINGER-SONGWRITER'S GUIDE TO RECORDING IN THE HOME STUDIO
by Shane Adams
00148211 Book $16.99

UNDERSTANDING AUDIO – 2ND EDITION
by Daniel M. Thompson
00148197 Book $24.99

SONGWRITING, COMPOSING, ARRANGING

ARRANGING FOR HORNS
by Jerry Gates
00121625 Book/Online Audio $19.99

BEGINNING SONGWRITING
by Andrea Stolpe with Jan Stolpe
00138503 Book/Online Audio $19.99

BERKLEE CONTEMPORARY MUSIC NOTATION
by Jonathan Feist
00202547 Book $17.99

COMPLETE GUIDE TO FILM SCORING – 2ND ED.
by Richard Davis
50449607 .... $29.99

CONTEMPORARY COUNTERPOINT: THEORY & APPLICATION
by Beth Denisch
00147050 Book/Online Audio $22.99

THE CRAFT OF SONGWRITING
by Scarlet Keys
00159283 Book/Online Audio $19.99

JAZZ COMPOSITION
by Ted Pease
50448000 Book/Online Audio $39.99

MELODY IN SONGWRITING
by Jack Perricone
50449419 Book $24.99

MODERN JAZZ VOICINGS
by Ted Pease and Ken Pullig
50449485 Book/Online Audio $24.99

MUSIC COMPOSITION FOR FILM AND TELEVISION
by Lalo Schifrin
50449604 Book $34.99

MUSIC NOTATION
PREPARING SCORES AND PARTS
by Matthew Nicholl and Richard Grudzinski
50449540 Book $16.99

MUSIC NOTATION
THEORY AND TECHNIQUE FOR MUSIC NOTATION
by Mark McGrain
50449399 Book $24.95

POPULAR LYRIC WRITING
by Andrea Stolpe
50449553 Book $15.99

SONGWRITING: ESSENTIAL GUIDE
Lyric and Form Structure
by Pat Pattison
50481582 Book $16.99
Rhyming
by Pat Pattison
00124366 2nd Ed. Book $17.99

SONGWRITING IN PRACTICE
by Mark Simos
00244545 Book $16.99

SONGWRITING STRATEGIES
by Mark Simos
50449621 Book $24.99

THE SONGWRITER'S WORKSHOP
Harmony
by Jimmy Kachulis
50449519 Book/Online Audio $29.99
Melody
by Jimmy Kachulis
50449518 Book/Online Audio $24.99